E. STANLEY JONES

&

SHARING THE GOOD NEWS IN A PLURALISTIC SOCIETY

GENERAL EDITORS

F. DOUGLAS POWE JR. AND JACK JACKSON

E. Stanley Jones and Sharing the Good News in a Pluralistic Society

The General Board of Higher Education and Ministry leads and serves The United Methodist Church in the recruitment, preparation, nurture, education, and support of Christian leaders—lay and clergy—for the work of making disciples of Jesus Christ for the transformation of the world. Its vision is that a new generation of Christian leaders will commit boldly to Jesus Christ and be characterized by intellectual excellence, moral integrity, spiritual courage, and holiness of heart and life. The General Board of Higher Education and Ministry of The United Methodist Church serves as an advocate for the intellectual life of the church. The Board's mission embodies the Wesleyan tradition of commitment to the education of laypersons and ordained persons by providing access to higher education for all persons.

Wesley's Foundery Books is named for the abandoned foundery that early followers of John Wesley transformed into a church, which became the cradle of London's Methodist movement.

E. Stanley Jones and Sharing the Good News in a Pluralistic Society

HIGHER EDUCATION & MINISTRY
General Board of Higher Education and Ministry
THE UNITED METHODIST CHURCH

CONTENTS

ACKNOWLEDGMENTS

We want to thank The Foundation for Evangelism for its support of the professorships and making this project possible. We also want to thank JillAnn Meunier for her editing and format work on this document.

FOREWORD

Jane Boatwright Wood

In 1984 the leadership of a small, United Methodist–affiliated foundation realized something that would ultimately change the way ordained clergy are prepared to serve our church. The Foundation for Evangelism (FFE) understood that having no required seminary training in evangelism failed to provide the church with the leadership required to fulfill the Great Commission's mandate to make disciples. Consequently, The Foundation dedicated its ministry to creating awareness in all church leaders that evangelism training is necessary. Later, when the General Conference of The United Methodist Church made evangelism training a priority, FFE positioned itself to facilitate the needed change.

The Foundation for Evangelism provides resources to equip and engage generations of Christian leaders—clergy and lay—to live out their passion for evangelism by inviting all people into a life-transforming relationship with Jesus Christ. Although the Wesley brothers never spoke of evangelism per se, they understood that personal holiness cannot, and should not, be separated from the practice of social holiness in the life of Christians and that both personal and social holiness inform our definition of evangelistic practices. Therefore, when FFE chose to commit its ministry and resources to support professors of evangelism at United Methodist-affiliated and Wesleyan-tradition seminaries around the world, they looked to the ministry of Brother E. Stanley Jones, who they believed best embodied their vision. Jones's innovative approach to evangelism—fusing evangelism and social responsibility—mirrors The FFE's evangelistic motivation.

In 1984 The FFE announced the E. Stanley Jones Professors of Evangelism initiative, and the first professor was placed at Boston University soon thereafter. In the ensuing years, E. Stanley Jones Professors of Evangelism have become integral members of the faculty at thirteen seminaries in the United States, Germany, Russia, and Zimbabwe. Over the last thirty-plus years, these exceptional academicians, mentors, and scholars have taught thousands of leaders how to better serve local churches and associated and extension ministries.

The FFE could not possibly have implemented, or even dreamed of, this program without the partnerships we enjoy with the thirteen seminaries. Together we have developed and refined expectations, so that those who serve in these chairs demonstrate the desire and address the church's need to equip capable, innovative leaders for our churches, communities, and world. In fact, the requirements are so rigorous that FFE also developed the Harry Denman Fellowship to meet the ongoing needs of these professors.

The synergy of all these components creates the possibility for this book. The principles of the Wesleys, the practices of Jones, and the scholarship of these scholars of evangelism are combined in this volume so that next-generation church leadership will be equipped to make disciples. The reader will see that, just as those of us who work so closely together in the E. Stanley Jones Professors of Evangelism program often comment, the stories and patterns of Jones's ministry are no less applicable today than when he first powerfully employed them.

INTRODUCTION

Jack Jackson

E Stanley Jones was perhaps the most significant missionary of the twentieth century. He was certainly the most influential Methodist missionary since Francis Asbury. While he is a relatively unknown figure today outside Methodist and missionary circles, from the 1920s through the 1960s he was a towering religious figure in many countries around the world, most notably the United States, Japan, and India.

Born in 1884 Jones experienced a conversion to Christianity when he was seventeen years old. Following graduation from Asbury College, Jones landed in India in 1907, at the age of twenty-three, as a missionary with the Methodist-Episcopal Church. His work as a missionary began as the English-speaking pastor of the Methodist Church in Lucknow. By the end of the 1930s his preaching ministry expanded to Iraq, Palestine, Egypt, Burma, Malaya, the Philippines, China, and Singapore. He was elected to the episcopacy of the Methodist-Episcopal Church in 1928 but withdrew his name the morning after his election.

By 1938 his influence was such that *Time* referred to him as "the world's greatest missionary." In the autumn of 1941 Jones worked tirelessly as a liaison between President Roosevelt and Japanese diplomats in an effort to keep the peace between the two countries (an effort that some argue almost avoided, and certainly postponed, the Japanese attack on Pearl Harbor).[1] He was asked to put his name forward in 1944 as the US Prohibition Party presidential candidate, which he rejected.[2] In 1962 Jones was nominated for the Nobel Peace Prize, and in 1963 he received the Gandhi Peace Prize. By 1964 *Time* said that only Billy Graham could rival Jones's international reputation. Presidents Roosevelt and Eisenhower, General Douglas MacArthur, John Foster Dulles, and Japanese Emperor Hirohito each sought Jones's advice in personal meetings and regular correspondence.

Jones's support of the Indian independence movement led him to be banished from India for a number of years. Concerns about communist sympathies led the FBI to develop a file on him.[3] He was a friend of Mahatma Gandhi, and Jones referred to Gandhi's murder as the greatest tragedy since the crucifixion of Christ.[4] On Jones's eightieth birthday, more than seventy-five thousand persons gathered from the Mar Thoma Syrian Church to celebrate his life and ministry in India.[5] Reinhold Niebuhr called him one of the great saints of his time.[6] By the end of his life Jones had published twenty-seven books, two of which sold more than one million copies. Yet one of his greatest contributions to the global community is often overlooked: his model of peaceful religious conversation among people with exclusivist religious convictions.

Much of the conversation today related to pluralism centers on the conviction that all religious truth claims are essentially contextual and relative. Diana Eck and Wesley Ariarajah are perhaps most representative of this opinion. The lines between religious traditions have been blurred, and claims of exclusivism and particularity are often marginalized. As a result, multireligious gatherings tend to include only people who share contemporary Western understandings of pluralism: while various religious traditions may differ in their external practices, the theologies that undergird them are similar. For example, Ariarajah argues the Trinity is not a uniquely Christian theological assertion but rather emblematic of various traditions, for the Trinity is not just Father, Son, and Spirit but also Brahma, Vishnu, and Shiva.[7] The goal of religiously plural conversations, therefore, becomes an effort to look past religious difference and to assert religious commonality in an effort to find common ground for peaceful work in the world today.

Jones certainly shared a commitment to peace, as is evident in his work with Gandhi, the Indian independence movement, and in his role as liaison between the United States and Japan. But his efforts did not flow from a conviction that all religions are different human expressions of a common commitment to one divine being. To the contrary, Jones's commitments flowed from a central conviction that Christ is the unique representation of God in flesh.

Jones was not a universalist. While he believed some from other religious traditions might be saved, their salvation is only through Christ's life, death, and physical resurrection. Jones's writing is frequently critical of the idea that all religious traditions are fundamentally the same, calling this view "mental abdication."[8] The belief that all faith traditions have the "same underlying truths," and that the "differences are in the details," tends to "wipe out distinctions, tone down superiorities, and have everything end in a diffused kindly feeling, or as someone has put it, 'in a mush of amiability.' All these things put together are disconcerting and disturbing."[9] Jones is clear in his belief that Jesus is the Son of God and the only hope for salvation in this life and the next: "The Name of Christ shall be above every name, not through propaganda, or any trick of fate, nor even through heavens' proclamations, but because it is inscribed in the constitution of our universe and in the make-up of our own souls."[10]

Jones wanted people to look at the "outlook, tendencies, and goals" of different faiths, not simply to identify "overlapping moral precepts and spiritual ideas."[11] When people from various traditions named their motivations and gave witness to their experiences of the divine, he believed that Christ would be made known, since only Christ offers a "vital" experience of God.[12]

Throughout this book the authors discuss a variety of practices that Jones incorporated into his ministry in India, which encouraged conversation among diverse people in plural communities. Three are especially important and are introduced briefly here: large-group evangelistic lecturing followed by a question-and-answer session, Round Table Conferences, and Christian Ashrams.[13] These three practices provide a model for true religious dialogue that is fundamentally peaceful and life-affirming. Jones's model necessitates the announcement of each religious tradition represented in a conversation, including the Christian tradition, so that each tradition has the opportunity to hear from the others and to make claims for the veracity of each tradition. While Jones clearly believed it was an opportunity for Christians to share their story and thereby evangelize, these practices also necessitated that Christians encounter other people's understanding of the "good news" found in their religious traditions. If truth was to be found elsewhere, Jones believed it should be embraced.

He sought truth wherever he might find it, a characteristic that made him quite willing to submit Christianity to the scrutiny of its critics. He sought conversation with persons from other traditions because, if there was a better representative of God than Christ, he wanted to know it. He believed that there are people in other traditions who, like him, sought truth and would want to hear what Christ had done in his life. He lived in a tension between the certitude of Christ's supremacy and a great openness to truth wherever he might find it.

In the end, though, he never discovered a more perfect representative of God than Christ. He never seemed to question the need for redemption from sin offered by Christ. His commitment to Christ, desire to share the good news he found in Christ, and openness to truth in other faiths led him to test his faith through the practice of public lectures, Round Table Conferences, and Christian Ashrams. Yet through the course of his life, he never encountered better news than the story of God redeeming the world in and through Jesus.

Public Lectures and Question-and-Answer Sessions

Despite the global nature of Jones's ministry, the epicenter of his work in the 1920s and 1930s was India. Even in the later decades of his life, when he spent more and more time in the United States, he continued to view India as his home. It was there that he developed the three practices.

The first point of contact between Jones and most Indians was in large, evangelistic lectures. Jones's public lectures followed a standard pattern. Events centered on a specific city for a week or weekend. Jones preached each morning in gatherings that were specifically designed for local Christian communities. Evening lectures focused on topics of interest to local intellectuals from other religious traditions. While the topics in the evening varied, they always included Jones sharing his experience of how faith in Christ affected his life. The entire event was facilitated or chaired by local persons, many of whom were not Christian. Lectures usually took place in public halls, open spaces, Hindu temples, or schools, but almost never in churches.[14] Each aspect of this standard pattern was designed to encourage persons from other religious traditions to come listen to the evening lectures.

A number of aspects of these public lectures are different from other large evangelistic gatherings of the day, both in India and around the world. First, Jones did not refer to them as "crusades" but as "lectures." Jones believed the term "crusade" was highly problematic, being so associated with Western imperialism, and the negative connotations could not be overcome. Second, while Jones usually spoke for 45–60 minutes, he rarely concluded with an evangelistic "call" to Christian faith as did other mass meetings of the day. Instead, he closed with a time of question-and-answer, which was followed by an invitation for anyone interested in hearing more about Christ to join Jones and others for further conversation. Questions were either submitted ahead of time or voiced in the public session.

While Jones would not critique other traditions in these question-and-answer sessions, many in the audience frequently critiqued his Christian faith. He welcomed this challenge, writing that his goal was to express his experience of Christ in the public lectures and then provide a venue for others to "break" it if they could.[15] These "grilling" sessions, as he called them, usually lasted between one and two hours.[16]

Third, Jones believed that his primary target was educated Indians. Reaching educated persons, typically men, was important to Jones, as he believed educated persons were often the people of greatest influence in a community. In turn, these influencers often persuaded entire communities to reject the story of Christ. Influencing these leaders to come to a place of Christian conversion was critical, he believed, to reaching a community as a whole. Jones's emphasis on reaching the educated stood in stark contrast to the mass Christian gatherings of the 1920s and 30s in India, which focused on encouraging poor populations to embrace the Christian faith.

Fourth, Jones's focus on educated populations also led to a focus on intellectual instead of emotional conversion, though he clearly believed emotions were part of the conversion experience. While a conversion might be very emotional, he believed conversion sprang from an intellectual journey. Jones believed that a true conversion, which includes both emotion and intellect, takes time.

His understanding of conversion as a journey is similar in this way to John Wesley's. Therefore, it is not surprising that Jones concluded these lectures with an invitation to further conversation about Christ, similar to John Wesley's practice in field preaching, in which he concluded not with an invitation to conversion as Whitefield did but rather with an invitation to Methodist society and class meetings. In these society and class meetings, conversations were encouraged that nurtured persons through personal doubts. Jones began these conversations in the question-and-answer sessions after public lectures.

Perhaps the immediacy of the question-and-answer sessions was necessary for Jones, since he typically spoke to groups of people who were from non-Christian communities and perhaps encountering Christianity for the first time. Consequently, in the question-and-answer sessions, Jones was frequently asked about Christianity's relationship with other faith traditions. Thus, the question-and-answer sessions after public lectures involved more conversations with non-Christian communities than Wesley's field preaching events usually did.

As we consider how Methodism today might converse with the world's non-Christian communities, we should remember that in these public lectures and question-and-answer sessions Jones refused to critique other religious traditions.[17] He concluded that debates strive to win arguments rather than discover truth.[18] Instead, he presented what he had discovered in Christ, and his experience of God through Christ, leaving others to form their own conclusions. He critiqued other traditions in print, arguing for Christ's uniqueness and supremacy over other religious traditions, but he did not do so in public lectures.

These large lectures were critical to gathering groups of people from other faith traditions who wanted to engage persons from the Christian faith. They became the first point of contact between Jones and people interested in Christ, providing a venue for initial conversations. But they did not offer the personal, long-term conversations that Jones thought most people require for true, lifelong conversion. More intimate conversations took place in the next two elements of his evangelistic ministry: Round Table Conferences and Christian Ashrams.

Round Table Conferences

The second key practice of Jones's evangelistic ministry, which also included significant conversations with non-Christian communities, was Round Table Conferences. The gathering usually consisted of between fifteen and forty people. Jones tried to ensure that approximately two-thirds of the participants were non-Christians, with the remainder being primarily Indian Christians. Everyone was asked to share only their religious experience and specifically "how religion was working, what it was doing for us, and how we could find deeper reality."[19] The focus was on the practical effect of faith in a person's life. The goal was to discover other people's actual experiences, not their understanding of dogma or doctrine. The focus must be "deeply experiential. What does religion bring in experience? What is its value for life?"[20] The focus of the conversations was not theology but the experiential benefits of faith.

The Round Table Conferences provided a venue for pointed conversations about different faiths, conversations where Jones believed an "untrammelled" Christ eventually stood at the center.[21] Round Tables were conversations among people from various religious traditions, secular philosophies, and ethical systems, who gathered as equals to share about their experiences of religion.

Jones wondered if the gospel he knew as a citizen of the United States would sound like the gospel in India. He writes:

> When we had stripped our [Christian] life of overgrown verbiage, how much fact would we have left? Would our gospel ring true to reality? Would it move amid these problems of life with assured poise and conscious power? Would it face life and answer it? Was our gospel a broken light from God illuminating patches and portions of life, but leaving unilluminated life as a whole? Or was it God's adequate answer to man's need-intellectual, moral, spiritual, and social?[22]

Indian communities were perhaps the best ones in which to ask these difficult questions of the gospel, for in it lived

> the most religiously inclined race of the world [containing] a people who have persistently searched for God and Reality as no other people on earth have searched. . . . What answer would they bring from that hoary past and this heaving present? Would it be an adequate one?[23]

The goal of the Conferences was then twofold: one, to bring together people from India's various religious traditions;[24] and two, to create a space for educated Indians to contemplate Christianity. In this way, the gatherings were both interreligious and evangelistic. Every person was invited to share around the table and, evidently, in only a handful of cases throughout the years did someone choose not to share.[25] The use of a round table was intentional, since nobody was the head of the meeting. Jones himself never started the sharing, and he resisted attempts to summarize or comment on other people's sharing. He usually shared at the end.

As at the lectures, the desire for the Round Tables was to steer away from debate and arguing. The goal was to have true conversation, sharing each person's experience. The result was that people from each tradition were challenged, even Christians, regarding the source and substance of their faith. Participants left with an "attitude of appreciation with appraisal" of all religious traditions.[26] Jones came to believe that these Round Table Conferences provided the greatest venue for true conversation between people of different faiths.

To be clear: Jones intended Christ to be central in Round Table Conferences. Participants certainly recognized that even though people from other traditions typically hosted the gatherings, it was a Christian (either Jones or someone from his ministry) who initiated and then led each Round Table Conference. Jones almost always spoke last, and while he tried not to sum up what others had said, he evidently was the person most people wanted to hear speak. I can find no evidence of him participating in a Round Table in which he was the only Christian voice or one that was clearly organized by people from other traditions.

Nevertheless these Round Table Conferences do seem to have had a remarkably hospitable and inclusive tone. Jones did want conversation, not monologue, and the only way to really encourage such dialogue was to give everyone, as much as possible, an equal seat at the table.

Christian Ashrams

While public lectures and Round Table Conferences were the two primary places for conversations among people of multiple religious and non-religious communities in Jones's ministry, Christian Ashrams also provided an important venue for even more intimate conversation. Jones's Christian Ashrams developed out of the Indian model of ashrams (good evidence that he was indeed willing to learn from other religious traditions and to indigenize the Christian faith).

Ashram literally means "apart from hard work." They are part of the Indian religious landscape. Jones's Ashrams were retreats, often lasting a week at a time. Jones eventually purchased multiple ashram locations, the first and most significant being at Sat Tal in 1930. While Hindu Ashrams typically center on a religious guru, Jones tried not to be the center of the retreat, though he was clearly the guiding figure.

The Christian Ashrams intentionally included people from various religious traditions, yet all participants were to have a "willingness to search sincerely for God's truth with other members of the Ashram on a basis of complete equality."[27] They became the place where people who had encountered Jones first in lectures, then engaged him and Christ more deeply in Round Table Conferences, could engage the actual practices of a Christian life in a concentrated and personal way.[28] These practices included worship, preaching, prayer, Bible study, Sabbath, and work. Discipleship and sanctification of believers were central to the Ashram movement, but Ashrams also provided an important venue for conversations with non-Christian communities to continue beyond public lectures and Round Table Conferences.

Lessons for Today

A number of theological foundations that undergird the practices of public lectures, Round Table Conferences, and Christian Ashrams are pertinent to Wesleyan conversations about interreligious engagement today. First, Jones believed in humanity's oneness. "The human heart and the human mind," he wrote, "are the same throughout the world . . . there are no permanently inferior or permanently superior races."[29] Today this may seem an unremarkable claim, but in India in the 1920s and 30s, when the caste system was still entrenched, it was remarkable. Out of this foundation of equality, Jones insisted that we are all children of God with the ability to live in community with God through Christ. Jones took this claim seriously, refusing to speak in segregated churches and colleges in the United States. He even resigned as a trustee of Asbury College when it refused to integrate. In the Christian Ashrams, the sign on meeting room walls read, "Leave behind all race and class distinction ye that enter here," a clear challenge to the ever-present caste system.[30] Jones's use of the words "brother" and "sister" was also a direct challenge to the caste system, not simply a reflection of Southern Evangelicalism in the United States.[31]

Second, Jones believed that God was at work in other religious traditions.[32] Christian traditions and the church were some of what he called Christ's "regular" channels. But, for Jones, the Spirit also operates through "irregular" channels, namely through activities and people who do not claim a Christian tradition yet who act in ways Jones believed to be fundamentally compatible with the person of Christ. For example, Jones believed that Gandhi embodied the principles of Christ.[33]

At the same time, Jones's relationship with Gandhi points to a third important principle in Jones's thought, namely his conviction that God in Christ offers a radically different vision of creation than is found in other faith traditions. Jones believed that Gandhi understood the principles of Christ but not the person of Christ.[34] In missing the person of Christ, Gandhi failed to see the uniqueness of what Jesus offers. Jones believed that all religions are not the same, and when truly and honestly compared, they point to different understandings of the divine and often offer contradictory visions of God's hopes for humanity and the purposes of the created order.

The differences among religions are one of the reasons Jones encouraged Round Table participants not to iron out differences between their beliefs.[35] Critique was not part of the Round Table, because Jones believed witnessing to what Christ has done in a person's life built bridges with people from other communities, creating a space where Christ would be inevitably revealed. Jones wrote that Round Table Conferences demonstrate that non-Christian faiths were "bankrupt," but he never seems to have said as much at a Round Table gathering.[36] In the personal space of public lectures, Christian Ashrams, and especially Round Table Conferences, the focus was experience rather than critique.[37]

Fourth, the Round Tables and Ashrams show that, for Jones, the task of evangelism is dialogical. It includes not only witnessing to our own faith, but a willingness to listen to others as they share their experiences of other faiths. When we listen to others they are more likely to listen to us. Furthermore, Jones believed that there was much to learn from the stories of different religions. Many other religious traditions offer some truth and life that Christians might need to incorporate into their own faith. Even in the case of religious or secular communities that might not offer any truth, the representatives who speak for them are children of God and thus deserve respect. For Jones, Christians cannot expect people of other religious traditions to listen to the Christian message if Christians are not willing to listen to the message of other religious traditions.

Conclusion

Jones's pattern of public lectures, Round Table Conferences, and Christian Ashrams set a model for how plural communities can engage in rich conversation. He believed in the uniqueness of the Christian faith, but his belief in the ability of all people to interact with the Holy Spirit led him to engage in open-ended conversations about the nature of various religious traditions and how people experienced the divine through them. His commitment to Christ was not a barrier to conversation with other traditions but opened him in dynamic ways to hearing other's faith stories, as well as sharing his own. His threefold evangelistic pattern of ministry, while highly specific to the context of India in the first half of the twentieth century, is an insightful model for Methodist communities in particular and Christian communities in general. It suggests how we can engage our religiously plural world with integrity, conviction, grace, humility, generosity, and openness.

"COME IN THE RIGHT WAY"

EFFECTIVE EVANGELISM IN PLURALISTIC CULTURES

Robert E. Haynes

The reality of religious pluralism in our world today is self-evident. Many Christians ask, "How can we share the gospel story (i.e., be evangelists) in a way that honors the other and builds a sense of community instead of animosity?" I believe E. Stanley Jones shows us a way. Jones's unique evangelism methods in his own profoundly religiously pluralist context provide important lessons for contemporary faith-sharing. The practices of evangelism that he incorporated into his ministry, especially his insistence that anyone who would seek to understand God needs only look to the person of Jesus Christ, inform contemporary efforts to share the gospel.

The Global Missionary Climate in the Early Twentieth Century

Jones arrived in India in 1907. He began his service amid a wave of missional movements, which had prepared a generation of missionaries who felt uniquely positioned to preach the gospel across the globe in an unprecedented way, and who believed they would see the conversion of the whole world by the end of their generation. This vision was reinforced by advances in technology, travel, and communication, which led many to believe that now was the opportune time for a globalized Christianity.

Jones's training for ministry would have likely emphasized some of the ideas expressed by the 1910 Edinburgh Missionary Conference. The delegates, drawn from several denominations, embraced a unified vision of mission, laced with militaristic overtones, which proclaimed that theirs was the hour in which the Christian movement would conquer the world.[1] It did not take long for Jones to recognize this sentiment in India. Writing in his 1925 work, *The Christ of the Indian Road*, he said:

> In the days when I volunteered to be a missionary the prevailing thought was that here is a cataract of human souls pouring into perdition and that we were to rescue as many as possible. Rightly or wrongly, this idea is no longer dominant as a motive for foreign missions.[2]

Though a global understanding of mission was still developing at this time, Jones found himself in a robust missionary environment. Stephen Graham wrote that "India was the 'most substantial and significant foreign mission enterprise.'"[3]

The Christ of the Indian Road is a compilation of Jones's recollections and accounts of his first seventeen years of ministry, as well as insights into his ministry in a pluralistic environment. Therein Jones mentions work among Hindus, Muslims, Buddhists, agnostics, and a variety of other sects. Moreover, the work was difficult, even where Christianity was already established. In some ways, India was already "conquered" by a "Christian army." Under British rule, given the close ties of church and government that came with such a rule, many in India saw Christianity as mere baggage that arrived with the conquerors.

Jones saw that the cultural overtones connected to Western

Christianity were a hindrance to his work. He described the culture, at least early in his ministry, as hostile to the Christian message because of the conflation many Indians made between the British rule and Christianity itself. The "name of Christ stood for all that India hated, for [Jesus] was identified with empire and the foreign rulers."[4] Christianity entangled in Western culture was such an obstacle to ministry in Jones's eyes that he sought to put as much distance as possible between it and his evangelistic message.

Evangelistic Methods of the Early Twentieth Century and Jones's New Vision

Jones identified three evangelistic methods that his contemporaries used in their efforts to address the plurality of faiths they encountered. One was what he called the "old method of attacking the weaknesses of other religions and then trying to establish your own on the ruins of the other."[5] The second was to show that the "ancient faiths" were fulfilled in Christianity, which Jones felt was an improvement on the first approach but needed further refinement. The third emphasized a discussion with non-Christians about a general subject that missionaries would steer to a distinctively "Christian message and appeal."[6] Though Jones saw some success in these efforts, he was not entirely comfortable appropriating them unchecked for his own ministry.

Jones said it was instinct that led him to explore new ways to evangelize in the environment of a variety of faiths. He originally outlined six principles in faith-sharing.

1) Frankness: he felt strongly that his audience should know that they were attending a faith-sharing event without camouflaging or hiding the purpose.

2) Humility: Jones would not attack another religion in his messages. "If there is an attack in [the message], it must be a positive presentation of Christ. He himself must be the attack."[7] This, he felt, would put the speaker and the hearer on equal footing: under the

17

judgment of Christ to adhere to the Christian message. In doing so, Jones was assuming a posture of self-effacement.

3) Openness: at the end of his messages, he welcomed difficult questions from his hearers.

4) Deference: the meetings were chaired by influential non-Christians.

5) Christ-centered: a key principle was his effort to define Christ outside of connotations that Christianity brought to Him. Therefore, he sought to remove the Western systems of church.

6) Experiential: Jones felt that "Christ must be interpreted in terms of the Christian experience rather than mere argument."[8]

Jones later added two more key principles to this list. First, he removed the term *Christianity* from his advertisements and discussions. Though his message remained Christ-centered, he vigorously sought to separate negative (often colonial) connotations of Christianity with the more positive vision of the Christ of Scripture.

Second, he emphasized that "Christ must be [presented] in an Indian setting."[9] He felt strongly that the gospel must be shared, as much as possible, in categories of the culture in which it finds itself. Jones lived in a pluralistic society that was suspicious of the Christianity of its colonizers. He ministered in a climate of, what he termed, a "growing national consciousness."[10] Such a consciousness embraced the pluralism of India's various religious backgrounds, while Christianity was perceived as the religion of the Western occupiers. Many in the growing nationalist movement saw Christian converts as traitors to the national cause of India. As the struggles for independence grew, so did the reticence to embrace the Christian faith. Jones's answer was to show that Christ walked the same Indian roads that His hearers did. As Jones puts it:

> Christianity to succeed must stand, not with Caesar, nor
> depend upon government backing to help, but must stand
> with the people. It must work with the national grain and

not against it. Christ must not seem a Western Partisan of
White Rule, but a Brother of Man.[11]

The success of Jones's work in India was reflected, not solely
in *how* he presented his message, but also *where* he presented his
message. Early in his missionary career Jones worked with the lower
castes of Indian society, as did many of his colleagues. The plight of
those in such castes was certainly difficult, and there was much work
to be done. However, Jones would leave the work in these groups at
the behest of a member of an upper caste.

Jones recalled a conversation with a government official that
changed the course of his ministry. The official requested that Jones
work among his peers, saying, "We want you to [work among us] if
you will come in the right way."[12] Though he was eager to take advan-
tage of such an opportunity to work among a key group of Indians,
he was overwhelmed by the stipulation to "come in the right way."
He felt intellectually inferior and unprepared to work with prominent
leaders amid growing nationalism.

The anxiety pushed Jones to a crisis point. Jones records that he
was in the middle of such a crisis when God intervened to give him
a renewed resolve for his missionary work and helped to define his
vision for work in the pluralistic upper classes. With this newfound
resolve he set out to engage the people of the various faith backgrounds he encountered from the upper castes. He sought to discover
where God was already working in their lives and point them to Christ
through those activities. One key way of doing so was his Round Table discussions.[13]

Round Tables were an important way for Jones to engage in the
discussion of faith with people from various faiths.[14] He put himself, a
Western Christian, firmly in the minority in such a setting. His *modus
operandi* was to invite approximately fifteen members of other faith
groups and five or six Christians to a Round Table. The majority of
Christians he invited were usually Indians. Typically, the participants

were highly educated and "really religious . . . the best representatives of the faiths we can find."[15] It was important to have such a "large preponderance of the members of other faiths not only because it gives wider range to the views expressed, but also in order that they may not feel that we Christians have packed the meeting."[16]

The Round Table discussions focused on two questions: "Have you found God?" and "Can you tell me how to find him?" In deference to his Indian hearers, Jones admitted that he borrowed these questions from Swami Vivekananda.[17] A product of his time, Jones encouraged his participants to engage the scientific method to experiment with, verify, and share the results of one another's religious experiences. The discussions were to be open and honest. Disagreements were not to be dismissed, but engaged as one might accept disagreements among family members. United Methodist missionary to India, Richard Taylor, said, "I know of nothing like this previously in India. [Prior discussion of faith in public] was usually either monologue or debate."[18]

The Round Table technique was one way for Jones to extricate the Christ he hoped to teach from the problems of the Western missionary Christianity, which, he felt, had confused the message he was trying to share. One such difficulty the Round Table was to overcome was the Western missionaries' unwillingness to learn from other religions or traditions. There was no room for a posture of superiority in such an environment. Jones shunned discussions of dogma and controversial issues. Instead, he sought to personalize the discussions by asking participants to consider the ways that religion has answered the important questions of life, including "its joys and its sorrows, its perplexities and its pains, the demands of duty, the moral struggle with sin and evil, the upwards call to higher life, the desire to help our fellow men and to be of use, [and] the craving for God."[19]

He encouraged his participants to avoid answering these questions in abstractions. He pushed them to give concrete accounts of their verified experiences of the truth, power, and redemption of God.[20] In maintaining the posture of a family discussion, Jones also instructed the participants to not shy away from their differences. He had no false pretenses that they would expect to find a "least common denominator . . . in Rama, or Krishna, or Buddha, or the Vedanta, or the Koran, or Christ."[21] Yet each was expected to participate with respect and regard for what the other had to share.

This revolutionary method for theological discussion became a hallmark of Jones's missionary work. It was foreign to the people of India but welcomed by many. Jones's obedience to God's call to work among a group previously overlooked, the upper castes of the educated and powerful, was profound. His humble posture was hitherto unseen among the Western missionaries. Jones himself realized just how radical such an approach was and that it was Christ who called him to utilize it. As he reminisced, it was a Hindu whom God used to give him the idea. "I am convinced that the nail-pierced hand of the Son of man [sic], through this son of the East, opened this door and bade us enter. It was a searching, dangerous adventure to which he called us."[22]

The Exclusivity of Christ

Jones rejected any sort of notion that pluralistic societies are fine without Christ. He writes, "I know of no one, East or West, who is getting along pretty well without Christ. Christ being Life is a necessity to life."[23] He also rejected the notion that Christ was a way among many other ways. He recalled a conversation with a Brahman who suggested he tailor his messages in such a manner that offered Jesus as one of several various paths. In doing so, Jones was told, he would win popularity; people would listen to his messages with more enthusiasm. Jones rejected such moves. He was compelled by what he knew to be true:

> It is a question of what are the facts. They have the final [word]. I should be glad, more than glad, if I could say that there are others who are saving [people], but I know of only One to whom I dare actually apply the term "Saviour."

But I do dare apply it to Christ unreservedly and without qualification.[24]

Though he was unwavering in his affirmation of the exclusivity of Christ for salvation, Jones was not afraid of the questions that other belief systems raised of his own faith. On the contrary, he embraced them. Jones recalled a time when a Hindu man called him a "broad-minded Christian." He replied, "My brother, I am the narrowest man you have come across. I am broad on almost anything else, but on the one supreme necessity for human nature I am absolutely narrowed by the facts to one—Jesus."[25] He furthered explained, "It is precisely because we believe in the absoluteness of Jesus that we can afford to take the more generous view of the non-Christian systems and situations. But the facts have driven us to Jesus as the supreme necessity for all life everywhere."[26]

Christ, Not Christianity

Jones was convinced that emphasizing the teachings of Christ, rather than of Christianity, would call his Indian hearers to judge their own beliefs by the Ideal rather than an interpretation thereof. He also learned that it exposed the exporters of the Christian message to this same judgment of Christ. Jones recalled a time when he had difficulty getting his message across to participants at a Round Table Conference. When he asked them why they were reticent to accept Christ, their answers were frank and charitable, but stinging. His audience wanted to know, if American civilization claimed to be Christian and claimed to live by such morals, why was there corruption in the government? If Christ taught love for all, why did "Christian" America have racially motivated lynching? If Christ is the Prince of Peace, why have "Christian" nations "not yet learned the way out of war?"[27]

The difficulties of such contradictions between Christ's message and the message of His followers emerged beyond the borders of the

United States. They were also present in the work of some Western missionaries to India. Jones was chagrined to see some of his contemporaries infected by racism and imperialism.[28] He provided two accounts of Indian nationals pointing out the discrepancy. First, he was told by an Indian philosopher, "Jesus is ideal and wonderful, but you Christians—you are not like him."[29] Second, he heard from a Hindu speaker at an academic lecture, "I see that a good many of you here are Christians. Now, this is not a religious lecture, but I would like to pause long enough to say that if you Christians would live like Jesus Christ, India would be at your feet tomorrow."[30] Such critiques contributed to Jones's resolve to expect his hearers to follow Christ alone rather than Christianity.

A proponent of enculturating Christ's message to the Indian context, Jones was unafraid to let Indian Christians bring with them the richness of their religious past, as long as Christ was the center of their religious expression. His emphasis on Christ incarnating in every culture reflects David Bosch's later sentiment that Christ will remain a "foreign entity" unless Christians bring him anew into a culture and let Him live in and through that culture.[31] Jones refused to allow himself, or the message of the Christian faith, to remain a foreign entity in India. Yet it would be a mistake to equate Jones's efforts with terms like "accommodation" or "adaptation." Such a notion would infer that he was merely rephrasing his message to allow his community to hear it in a new way. Jones embraced a Christian expression that allowed for some cultural pluralism, though he refused to waver on the centrality of Christ.

Lessons for Today

Contemporary evangelists are faced with issues of globalization that Jones could not have imagined. It is not necessary to move to India to find enough people to hold a Round Table dialogue of educated people from various religions to discuss issues of faith. Members of such groups can be found in nearly any American community: at the local park, corner coffee shop, or even on a smartphone or tablet. The proliferation of news and information can also invite us into conversations that would have otherwise been out of reach to many just a decade ago. National discussions in the West around issues of immigration, race, and religion have far-reaching implications that are tilting the global axis.

American culture is politically, culturally, and religiously plural. Political pluralism is celebrated, and necessary, when it forces parties to balance power and prevent absolute authority in one person or party.[32] Cultural pluralism embraces a range of cultures within a nation and provides for the mutual amelioration of the citizens of that nation. A nation is enriched when a variety of gifts, talents, and customs are present. Much of the discussion on religious pluralism in the United States has centered upon the legal and civic ramifications of a constitutional right to the freedom of religion.[33]

Data from the Pew Research Center indicate that while 89 percent of Americans reported a belief in God, the practice of that belief is far from monolithic. Most of the "religiously affiliated population" is represented by "a wide variety of Protestants as well as Catholics."[34] Members of other faith groups—such as Jewish, Muslim, Hindu, and Buddhist adherents—are a significant influence in the United States, though their relatively small numbers by percentage may not directly reflect such influence. Meanwhile, the number of those who report no religious preference is growing; there are as many "nones" as Protestants among adults under thirty years of age.[35] However, the discussion of religious pluralism needs more careful articulation than just a recitation of numbers and a list of groups. Certainly, there is a wide variety of philosophies in each of these belief systems. Additionally, the dynamics of the growing percentage of the population that describe themselves as "spiritual but not religious" is yet to be understood by researchers.[36] There are pluralities inside the pluralities and growing societal pressure to accept each of these as equal to one's own beliefs.

What, then, can E. Stanley Jones's work teach contemporary Christian missionaries and Christians who find themselves in a pluralistic culture? I suggest four ideas to "come in the right way":

First, we should assume a posture of humility. Jones's approach to the Round Tables won him several hearers. He did not directly contest the beliefs of the members of those discussions but instead invited them into a dialogue about deeper matters. The discussion of these deeper matters provided him the opportunity to show them what they had been looking for all along but may not have realized: Christ Himself.

> [People] wonder if there can be a good God . . . when they see earthquakes wipe out the innocent and guilty alike and innocent little children suffer from nameless diseases they did not bring on themselves. But the distracted and doubting mind turns towards Jesus with relief and says, "If God is like that, he is all right." As Christians we affirm that he is—that he is Christlike in character, and we say it without qualification and without the slightest stammering of the tongue. We believe "God is Jesus everywhere" and Jesus is God here—the human life of God.[37]

Second, we should focus on Christ instead of Christianity and Christian traditions. Jones recognized the difficulties that the British rule and Western missionary fervor brought to his work. He led the move to disconnect Westernized models of church from the message of Christ for his Eastern hearers. As Jones put it, "I am frank to say that I would not turn over my hand to westernize the East, but I trust I would give my life to Christianize it. It cannot be too clearly said that they are not synonymous."[38] By "Christianize it" he means that all would enter into a saving relationship with Christ but not necessarily adopt all of the trappings of Western nations that claimed to be founded on Christianity. Jones rejected the notion of a "Christian nation." He clearly believed people, and even communities of people, became identifiably Christian but not a nation as a whole: "There are

Christianized individuals and groups, but the collective life of no people has been founded upon the outlook of Jesus."[39]

Such a posture is helpful in contemporary faith-sharing as well. The United States remains removed from the Christian ideal. Some politicians who profess Christian moral fortitude fall victim to corruption and scandal. Some church leaders commit crimes against even the most vulnerable. Social ills remain, due in part to the inactions of those who would profess a Christian outlook but do not embody it. In such a culture it is little wonder that the number of those who claim to be "spiritual but not religious" is on the increase.

Jones found himself among many who sought a spirituality but who wanted to distance themselves from the negatives of those who proclaimed the Christian message. As best he could, Jones sought to separate the two; the Message that is Christ from the impediments of those who would claim to be His messengers. Just like those in Jones's India, those in the contemporary culture look for answers to questions beyond themselves, as the Pew Research mentioned above pointed out. Most of them proclaim to believe in God, but that belief is expressed in a variety of ways. Some look for God among organized religious groups such as Hinduism, Buddhism, Islam, and the like. Some are seeking to prioritize themselves in their spiritual lives with a "sacralized self."[40] These notions, according to Jones, could be addressed by providing the answer to a question that many may not even be aware they were asking. As he put it: "The greatest news that has ever been broken to the human race is the news that God is like Christ. And the greatest news that we can break to [the] non-Christian world is just that—that the God whom you have dimly realized, but about whose character you are uncertain, is like Christ."[41]

Third, we should minister to a variety of populations. As noted above, many of Jones's contemporary missionaries were working with the lower castes of Indian society. However, Jones felt a distinct call to work among those who were not necessarily financially poor but nevertheless spiritually impoverished. He saw that those among the intellectual class needed to hear of the saving love of Jesus Christ just as much as anyone else. He wanted all people to have a chance at the abundant life in Christ he had discovered. He stood on the premise that only Christ could provide that for them.[42] Jones's openness to missionary work to those who were otherwise underserved, and still in need of a presentation of the gospel, serves as a guide for ministry among similar populations.

Fourth, we should maintain a clear emphasis on the centrality of Christ for salvation for all people. Though Jones did not directly attack religious pluralism, he did not allow a consilience that can easily slip into universalism. He had no place for universalism in his missionary theology or activity.[43] Jones was not afraid to share a "narrow" Christian message as broadly as possible. He sought to engage his hearers' minds and hearts with the message of Jesus as Savior:

> If this whole question of missions is to hold the affections of the church in the future, we must be sure that we are about a business that commends itself to the mind as well, for what does not hold the mind will soon not hold the heart. Besides, let it be noted that if Christianity isn't worth exporting it isn't worth keeping. If we cannot share it, we cannot keep it.[44]

Though he himself was humble in his approach to ministry, Jones remained the "narrowest man" when it came to the proclamation of Jesus as God. As we have seen, he was insistent that such absoluteness facilitated his generous view of other religions. To people who searched for the divine, Jones was ready to show them what they sought. As he investigated the facts, and revealed those facts to his audiences, he showed that they lead to Jesus Christ. Jones sought to convey this message in such a way that his Indian hearers could see Jesus in their own context, not always bound by the trappings often associated with Western historical Christianity. He sought to show his hearers that Christ walked their streets, stood among their crowds, healed their sick, announced the good news of the Kingdom of God among them, died upon the cross for them, and walked those streets again in resurrected form. This was his answer to the charge to "come in the right way." This he called "the Christ of the Indian Road," and it was this image of Christ that would be his goal in conversations among the pluralities of religious adherents he would encounter.[45] The lesson remains the same for contemporary Christians who seek to minister in pluralistic cultures.

CHRIST, KINGDOM, AND CHURCH

E. STANLEY JONES ON ECCLESIOLOGY AND NEW ECCLESIAL COMMUNITY

Jeffrey A. Conklin-Miller

It might be said that in his life and ministry E. Stanley Jones sought to "gaze at Jesus Christ" but only to "glance at the earthen vessel—the church which contains this Treasure."[1] The centrality of Christ and Kingdom is well known in Jones's work and provides the foundation for his initiatives in mission and ministry. Of particular interest in this chapter is his development of the Christian Ashram as a parachurch renewal movement. Even so, Jones wrote much more about Christ and Kingdom than he did about the church.

Given the historical failures of the church to reflect its high calling as the Body of Christ and the "sign, instrument, and foretaste" of the Kingdom of God, the theological distinction and recognized tension between church and Kingdom is not difficult to accept.[2] However, the distinction can be overstated, to the point of creating a divide between "church" on the one hand and "mission" on the other. Put simply, ecclesiology is pitted against missiology.

From within the church, there can be a "deep distrust of those

whose center of gravity is in mission, with the concern that such people are in danger of 'dumbing down' on church and its traditions."[3]
However, for those who seek first the Kingdom of God, "there is a
great concern that Church can institutionalize and withdraw Christians from real connection and involvement in the world outside the
'bubble' of the Church."[4]

Even so, in this chapter, I will argue that from the foundation of
Christ and Kingdom Jones's work in the Christian Ashram can draw
attention to the nature, structure, and mission of the church, perhaps
inadvertently, in helpful and instructive ways. More specifically, I will
suggest the Christian Ashram might be better viewed as a radical
embodiment of Christ and Kingdom that constitutes an innovative
ecclesial community, a new or perhaps "fresh expression" of church.[5]
In this frame, I believe Jones's theological and practical contribution
bridging Christ, Kingdom, and church may be instructive to those
seeking to lead in the work of ecclesial innovation today.

Pursuing this, I will begin with a short consideration of Jones's
core commitments to Christ and the Kingdom of God and then turn
to consider the Christian Ashram—particularly how such a model of
Christian life might reflect, for Jones, not only an embodied community of the Kingdom of God but also a truer vision of what church is
called to be. In a final section, I will consider the contribution Jones
makes to contemporary reflection on communities of ecclesial innovation. I suggest that Jones helps us see that the Kingdom and
church, ecclesiology and missiology, must dwell closely together in
the imagination of those engaged in forming ecclesial communities
in the future.

Jesus Christ (The Unchangeable Person)

Jones sees the church as "the greatest serving institution on earth"
that "has many critics but no rivals in the work of service to humanity."[6] This is demonstrated in the church's work to develop programs
and initiatives to serve the causes of education, health care, and

support for the disabled; in fact, "everything to lift the soul, the mind, the body of the human race."[7] However, this work should first be viewed as the fruit of a more primary, fundamental activity rooted in the power of changed or transformed character; and second, seen as originating in the transformation that comes only through engagement with Christ.

Consequently, this focus on Christ constitutes the first significant move to make when trying to articulate Jones's sense of the church and ecclesiological vision. When we speak of the Body, we must begin by clarifying whose body we are discussing—the Body of Christ. Jones writes:

> Jesus Christ is the center of worth and hope of the Christian church. We have this treasure in an earthen vessel. Don't point to the earthen vessel—its cracks, its outworn inscriptions, its outworn shape, its unmodern appearance, but rather look at what it holds. It holds the person of Jesus Christ.[8]

In truth, Jones's relationship to the earthen vessel of the institutional church was complicated. His early ministry in pastoral and supervisory/superintending roles led to mental and physical breakdowns, so that after his first seven years of ministry, Jones did not actively seek denominational or ecclesial leadership positions within established structures.[9] In fact, although he was elected bishop in 1928, he resigned the day after the appointment, reporting later the reaction of a pastor with whom he shared the news: "'Thank God,' the pastor said. 'Many of us thought a mistake had been made when they made you into an executive when you were an evangelist and a missionary.'"[10]

Despite any concern with the structures of the institutional church, Jones's greater interest was working out an appropriate theological foundation for his missionary activity in a non-Western context. In the evangelistic work of missionary activity and interfaith engagements, Jones begins with Christ. More specifically, he focuses on the "disentangled Christ"—which is to say, the person of Jesus Christ—but without appealing to His embodiment in either "Western civilization" or in the "Christian Church."[11] He states, "Christianity has its creeds, but it is not a creed; it has its doctrines, but it is not a doctrine; it has its rites and ceremonies, but it is not a rite or ceremony; it has its institutions, but it is not an institution. At its center, it is a person. Christianity is Christ."[12] Thus, this "disentangled" Christ is the pivot for everything concerning the church, and ecclesiology must begin with Him. But while we speak of Jesus Christ and Christ's mission, Jones emphasizes that we must also speak of the Kingdom of God—a kingdom fundamental to the identity, nature, and mission of the church.

Kingdom of God (The Unshakable Foundation)

To know E. Stanley Jones's theological vision is to know the central importance of the Kingdom of God. To speak of the Kingdom, however, does not take focus away from the importance of the Person of Jesus Christ—for to speak of the Person inevitably leads us to focus on the Kingdom, as they are essentially one and the same. As Jones writes, Jesus "'went out preaching the gospel of the kingdom,' Himself the meaning and illustration of that kingdom. He used interchangeably 'for my sake' and 'for the kingdom's sake.'"[13]

The close framing of Jesus and the Kingdom made clear that, for Jones, the Kingdom of God could not be simply an unrealized vision of a future reality. Nor could the Kingdom be viewed as existing only in spiritual or nonphysical space. Instead, Jones insisted, the Kingdom of God should be seen in realistic and realized terms—a present reality and possibility—and as such, as impacting everything; for in the Kingdom of God, "the economic, the social and political, the physical, and moral and spiritual, and the collective were to be redeemed."[14] The vision of the Kingdom of God is a holistic vision, leaving nothing out.[15]

To focus on the holistic nature of the Kingdom of God, therefore, is to draw attention to the current social reality that falls short of this ideal vision:

> The kingdom of God is the most radical conception ever presented to the human race . . . it meant nothing less than the replacement of this present unworkable world order, founded on greed and selfishness and exploitation, with God's order founded on love and service and mutual aid. There is a tension set up between the two.[16]

Additionally, this was a tension between not only the Kingdom and the world but also the Kingdom and the church, and it informed what the church is called to do and to be.

For Jones, the redemptive purpose of God is articulated in Jesus ("Unchangeable Person"), and in the community he creates ("Unshakeable Kingdom"), with the hope of transformation not only for individuals, or for "souls" in search of a deeper "spiritual life." In fact, what God reveals in Christ and Kingdom is the hope for the world, embedded in the very order of creation, or as he describes it, "the grain of the universe," meant for establishment in the world now, in history, in reality.[17] As Jones writes:

> There is something at the heart of the universe which is working for Christ and with Christ: those who align themselves to that something are in alignment with the redemptive purposes of the universe, and they go up in proportion to that alignment or they go down as they depart from it.[18]

In other words, written into the pattern of creation itself, God's redemptive purpose will not be thwarted by a lack of participation or faithfulness by the church. In fact, Jones suggests that the possibility of participation in God's redemptive purpose is not limited to Christians or to the church: "I do not mean to say that living according to Christ is confined to those within the Christian church. The Christian spirit has gone beyond the Christian church."[19] As a result, given the Spirit's work beyond the confines of the church, "anyone anywhere, inside or outside the Christian church, who consciously or unconsciously lives according to Jesus Christ," participates in God's redemptive activity.[20]

Christ, Kingdom, and Church

That said, for Jones, there is no question that the church is called to be the primary location for the operation of God's redemptive agenda in the world. Put differently, we might say Jones fully believes that the church is called to be the "sign" of the Kingdom of God and the "instrument" by which the Kingdom of God is made increasingly real in creation.

In one of his most explicit reflections on the nature and structure of the church, Jones draws from his holistic vision of the Kingdom of God. The church, he argues, must be a community or a society that meets the world's deepest needs through the work of embodied care for others, without limits, "beyond self, family, class, race, and creed. It must be a care universal—even for enemies."[21] In this fashion, the church is, in fact, God's instrument; and to the extent that the church reflects this grounding in Christ and Kingdom, it not only fulfills its purpose, but more significantly, it participates in the redemptive purpose of God in the world.

Yet, when it comes to its role of embodying God's redemptive program, Jones acknowledges that the church fails more often than it succeeds. This tension was particularly pronounced in Jones's reaction to the gathering of the Tambaram International Missionary Conference near Madras in 1938. On the eve of world war, in a gathering of both "older" and "younger" churches, Jones advocated for a vision of church closely aligned with and in service to the Kingdom of God. The results of the conference, however, left him sorely disappointed. Writing about the meeting, Jones was clear in his critique of not only the conference but also the church:

> It [the conference] blazed no great way. Why? Because of
> its basic starting point—the Church. It began there and

worked out to all its problems from the Church standpoint "The Church is the world's greatest hope!" That is not a chance sentence. It sums up the presuppositions of Madras. . . . Is the Church the hope of the world? If so, God help us! . . . God is laying hold of other instruments besides the Church to realize the Kingdom of God.[22]

The church, for Jones, is a disappointment when it comes to embodying Christ and a way of life reflective of His Kingdom: "We cannot put our full weight down on the church" because "if we do, it lets us down. We can only put our full weight down on Christ and the Kingdom."[23] If the church could not or would not fulfill its calling to be more than just the "sign" or the "instrument" but rather an actual "foretaste" of the Kingdom of God, then Jones must turn in another direction to find the embodiment of God's redemptive purpose in Christ and Kingdom—a direction that points to his experimental ecclesial work, particularly in the development of the Ashram movement, to which we now turn.

Christian Ashram: Ecclesial Innovation

As we have already seen, Jones's foundational commitment to the centrality of Christ and a radical vision of the Kingdom of God led him to a dim view of the contemporary Western church, which, in his estimation, failed more than it succeeded to reflect these same commitments. While Jones continued to maintain his commitment to the church, as the "home" for all Christians, and while he articulated frameworks within which the unity of the church might be strengthened, he also began to form communities that reflected and enacted life in the way of Christ and His Kingdom.[24] In this section I will examine Jones's development of the Ashram movement, not only as a force for renewal in the church, but as a form of ecclesial experimentation. Grounded in Christ and Kingdom, the Ashram community can be a helpful model to inform contemporary conversation and to

35

shape broader imagination about the shape of the church now and in the future.

Grounded in his experience of the Methodist class meeting, the Ashram was conceived by Jones as a community of truthful sharing, loving accountability, and authentic Christian living.[25] Adapting the traditional Hindu practice of ashram, wherein "religious disciples seeking salvation practice disciplined corporate living under the guidance of a guru, or teacher," Jones developed a community that sought to overcome the various barriers erected to create and maintain social differences and that functioned to disrupt life in harmonious community.[26] This emphasis on developing true "corporate life" led to the establishment of group decision-making, emphasizing discernment and consensus building, with particular efforts made to include the voices and perspectives of all members of the community.[27] Gossip and "secret criticism" were eschewed, replaced with honest expressions of truth in a daily gathering of the "Family Meeting" where differences and issues in relationship could be worked through toward clarity and reconciliation.[28]

Establishing such a communal life also required the overcoming of various types of distinctions and "barriers" that impeded the formation of a life together. "If the group is to be the Kingdom," Jones wrote, "then we must get down barriers, for the Kingdom is God's redemptive invasion of us."[29] "So," Jones goes on to spell out the implications of the embodiment of this radical standard, "we get down the barriers of race and class . . . we will not go where all races and all classes cannot come together on the basis of complete equality."[30] Participants in the Ashram community all bore the title "brother" or "sister" to emphasize their equality, and efforts were made to include the oldest and the youngest members together, resisting differentiations defined by age.[31]

Economic barriers were also to be overcome in the Christian Ashram. From the beginning, Jones introduced practices in the community that disrupted established norms defined by distinctions of class or (given the context) caste. He writes that those involved "felt we should take the New Testament basis, 'Distribution was made according to each one's necessities,' as the basis of our corporate living."[32] Rather than accepting divisions among laborers, all in the Ashram shared in work to sustain the community.[33] In all these ways, overcoming barriers and establishing the ways of life that build community, Jones creates in the Ashram a context for the rehearsal of the Kingdom of God.[34]

Even so, Jones was quite clear that the Ashram did not seek to be a church. Nor was it meant to be anything other than "church-centered," to the extent that the life the Ashram might shape in participants might lead to a deeper commitment to Christ and Kingdom. In this way, Jones saw the Ashram as a "permeative movement," having a strengthening effect within congregations and throughout the church.[35]

In this way, then, the Ashram movement plays the role of renewal movement within the larger structure and life of the church, the *ecclesiola* within the *ecclesia*. And, as a parachurch organization, the Ashram joins other movements, retreats, and organizations seeking to strengthen or intensify faithful Christian commitment, while not threatening the given institution of church or congregation.

However, the Ashram can be considered not solely as a parachurch movement seeking evangelical renewal in the larger, institutional church but also as a form of radical Christian community, and, in this way, an experiment in ecclesial innovation. Therefore, it is possible that Jones himself saw that the Ashram was closer to what church was truly meant to be than was the institutional, denominational church.[36] Such a conclusion might be based first on Jones's own distinction made between the "body" and the "soul" of the church, drawing focus to the *koinonia* at the heart of the church; and second, on the way the Ashram reflected his radical commitments to a realized Kingdom of God. Put succinctly, to the extent that it embodies *koinonia* and Kingdom, the Ashram can be what a congregation and denomination cannot be: namely, truly *church*.

First, let us consider the soul that enlivens the body of the church: *koinonia*, or "fellowship." Jones suggests, based on the biblical account in the book of Acts, that *koinonia* is a more fundamental concept than church. At Pentecost, he points out, it is not the church that is formed, as "the church is not mentioned in Acts until the eighth chapter." Rather, "it was the koinonia which was born out of Pentecost, for the koinonia is mentioned in the same chapter with the coming of the Holy Spirit."[37] Given its relationship to the Spirit's creative activity, this community is unlike others demonstrated in the establishment of an inclusive fellowship "across all barriers of race and class and sex and age."[38] In short, Acts describes a *koinonia* community of the Spirit where all are welcomed, barriers are broken down, and unity is established in Christ and a realized Kingdom.

Notably, the appearance of this *koinonia* does not necessarily translate into the appearance of the church. As Jones clarifies, "Where you have the koinonia, you have the church; where you do not have the koinonia, you have an organization, but not the church, except in name."[39] The distinction is important, because it clarifies the need for a movement like the Ashram that seeks (again, in Jones's words) "to put the koinonia back into the church."[40] While Jones doesn't make any claim as to the ecclesial status of the Ashram, his argument makes room for others to make the case that the Ashram, as it embodies *koinonia* in actual contexts, may more closely approximate something called church.

To strengthen this claim, we need to consider how the Ashram actually embodies a way of life that reflects or approximates, for Jones, what church is truly called to be, namely, "the Word of the kingdom become flesh—a kingdom in miniature."[41] As we have already seen, for Jones, such a commitment leads well beyond any disembodied or spiritualized interpretation, as life in the Kingdom of God requires the overcoming of real, historical barriers that divide, addressing and undoing inequalities of race, class, caste, profession, and so on. The Ashram does not necessarily point to the church or to another location or embodiment of the Kingdom; instead, the Ashram seeks to *be* that location. As Stephen A. Graham has put it, "For Jones the Christian ashrams were the consummate expression of the kingdom of God."[42] While Jones surely would not claim that the Ashram was commensurate to church, there are reasons to believe he might have seen it closer to the ideal than the congregational and denominational machine that bore the ecclesial title at that time.

That said, it must be acknowledged that because Jones did not intend Ashram to be church, he does not take responsibility to articulate anything like a fully developed ecclesiology, attending to orders of ministry, credal marks, or, most notably, sacramental life. As a result, the Ashram movement stood (and continues to stand) in the space allotted to intra-denominational renewal movements or as a parachurch organization. But in a final section I wish to consider the important contribution that Jones's theological and practical/experimental work in the Christian Ashram might make to contemporary conversations around the formation of new ecclesial communities.

Lessons for Today: Forming Innovative Ecclesial Community

Here I want to bring into the conversation the radical ecclesial vision of E. Stanley Jones and some of the contemporary reflection on forming new ecclesial communities. Specifically, from Jones, leaders of contemporary experiments in forming new ecclesial communities should remember the calling to be a "foretaste" of the Kingdom of God. Thus, such a calling can be grounded only in a community— such as the Christian Ashram—formed on the theological foundations that Jones drew attention to—namely, Christ and the Kingdom of God. It is through such basic commitments we are led to attend to inclusion and equality, thereby overcoming the social, racial, economic and other barriers that stratify human communities.

39

This is an important offer to new ecclesial communities that struggle to resist the temptation to form community life only on the basis of appearing attractive to lapsed Christians, non-Christians, and the so-called "nones."[43] In fact, the formation of human community into niche markets may have its appeal; but the assembling of what are, in effect, consumers around the axis of shared interests may have little that is properly Christian about it. Of course, contextualization calls for careful listening and the formation of community through shared discernment and locatedness; but without a certain set of basic Christian commitments, such communities will ultimately lack tethers to hold them to the center that is Christ.

The role of such tethers may be to shape new forms of ecclesial community as not only "signs" or "instruments," but actual, historical, embodied "foretastes" of the Kingdom of God. This is important in the contemporary moment, as Bishop Graham Cray has argued, because the image of the church as a "foretaste" of the Kingdom is the image that "best helps define its missionary task at a time of cultural change."[44] The "foretaste" offered by the church brings hope, which is a missing quality in "Western, affluent, multi-choice cultures," according to Cray.[45] The church offers an alternative only when it can be distinct enough from such cultures so as to offer a "foretaste of the future Christ has secured for that part of his creation within the new heavens and earth"[46]

The challenge Jones poses, therefore, is the challenge to evaluate ecclesial experiments as they succeed or fail to embody the characteristics of a true *koinonia*. More specifically, Jones might ask to what extent particular communities actually practice a way of life that truly sustains inclusion and equity across social and cultural differences, modeled by Christ and emblematic of His Kingdom program. Such a community would itself appear to be "different" from its context, not so as to be unintelligible, but rather, different enough to constitute an alternative offer.

Reflecting Jones's commitments, Rowan Williams offers a set of questions ecclesial communities might utilize to evaluate life together and to discern the shape of a faithful witness.[47] Such questions may be helpful frames for the ways Jones's own witness can continue to challenge and to form our own ecclesial imagination.

First, Williams asks, "How does the community enable its members to grow in prayer so as to enter more fully into the central mystery of Christ's relationship with his Father?"[48] Participation in the life of God is the starting point. In prayer and, presumably, all Christian practices, particularly sacramental ones, the community is invited to the fundamental connection between Christ and His Body, the church.

Second, Williams calls attention to the nature of the community's inner life and asks, "How far does the community encourage and enable its members to teach and to learn from one another?"[49] The mutuality required for such an exchange in this particular form of community would call for attention to the overcoming of barriers in imagination and in structure that would inhibit such activity. Put differently, the ecclesial community must be a community of inclusion and equity, such as that we have seen Jones envision through the Christian Ashram.

Third, and perhaps most important, new ecclesial communities are invited to consider whether

> the community [can] point to something in its collective life that makes a contribution to the wider society which would not be made if there were no Christian presence around? In other words, can it point to a distinctive practice that shows in some area of public life that there are alternative ways of managing human relations or problems to the ones that prevail most widely in our culture? The point is simply to show that there is *something* specific that is happening as a result of Christian commitment locally that can be pinned clearly to a set of distinctive convictions about how human relations should flourish.[50]

This third question invites new ecclesial communities to consider how their life together might offer a foretaste—a realized, historical, embodied Christ and Kingdom. We can hear the echo of Jones's voice calling church leaders to attend, not only to the inner life of the community, but to the public witness the community offers through the shape of its inner life. Jones's hope for conversion is focused on not only a personal, transformational experience but also the hope of a converted culture, society, and world.

In the end, Williams's questions for new ecclesial communities also reduce (but do not eliminate) the tension that exists between the church and the Kingdom of God. With Jones, the radical nature of Kingdom life cannot be lost in new forms of innovative ecclesial community. But, over and above what Jones was able to articulate, such communities must also remain truly ecclesial—they should aspire to be expressions of the church.[51]

Conclusion

In this chapter I have tried to show that, despite his concern with and critique of the church, E. Stanley Jones's theological and practical vision can be seen to do some important ecclesiological work. Specifically, Jones helps us to see that a community called to be the church must first be a community of Christ, embodying His Kingdom. Rather than dividing ecclesiology from missiology, Jones's vision can help keep these conversations connected, not to collapse the church into the Kingdom (or vice versa), but instead to better articulate the vocation of the church as sign, instrument, and foretaste of the Kingdom of God.

This offer comes at an important moment as a new generation of planters and pioneers embraces the calling to mission in the formation of new and innovative ecclesial communities. Will these communities resist the temptation of market forces that would see them shaped only as gatherings for like-minded consumers with shared interests? Or will they be communities that overcome barriers established by the world and offer a space increasingly unique, where inclusion and equity are more than just ideas and future ideals? Jones challenges us and expands our imagination at just this point. Reflecting on his ministry, Jones wrote, "The three things I needed were: an unshake-able kingdom, an unchangeable person, and both as realism."[52] In this frame, Jones offers a crucial foundation for the ongoing work of forming new ecclesial communities.

VICTORY THROUGH SURRENDER

E. STANLEY JONES'S UNDERSTANDING OF CONVERSION

Joon-Sik Park

[Conversion] is the vital fact that the church must bring or fail. When the church loses its power to convert, it loses its right to be called a church . . . it is failing as a church of the living Christ.

—E. Stanley Jones, Christ at the Round Table

E Stanley Jones was one of the most prominent American missionaries of the twentieth century, and he had significant influence on missionary thinking and practice. Central to his comprehensive vision of Christian mission was an integral understanding of and unyielding commitment to conversion. He was acutely conscious that human need and sin are without geographical bounds or distinctions and that the deepest human need is conversion. He thus committed his "life to reconciliation"—between God and humans and between humans themselves—"worldwide among all races and tribes and peoples."[1]

Convinced that "there is no such thing as a Christian nation,"[2] Jones considered not only the East but also the West as his mission field. He was mindful that conversion and church membership do not fully overlap each other. In his autobiography, written at the age of eighty-three, he shared:

> I have come to the conclusion that two thirds of the peo-
> ple in churches need conversion. Only one third know at
> firsthand what conversion really is. It is that one third that
> keep the soul of the church alive. The two thirds then are
> a field for evangelism instead of a force for evangelism. I
> have therefore spent more than half of my life in trying to
> convert unconverted church members."[3]

Jones found the church in the West largely anemic and came to embrace "Christianiz[ing] unchristian Christianity"[4] as part of his evangelistic work.

This chapter seeks to examine Jones's view of human nature and the human problem by taking a close look at his understanding of Christian conversion. A holistic theology of conversion with a clear understanding of human nature would be essential for producing a life and witness of wholeness. In E. Stanley Jones, we find a vision of conversion in which personal, ecclesial, and social transformations are integrally held together.

Jones's Understanding of Human Nature

Discussing the law of love in politics and economics in his *An Interpretation of Christian Ethics*, Reinhold Niebuhr wrote:

> The unvarying refrain of the liberal Church in its treatment
> of politics is that love and cooperation are superior to con-
> flict and coercion, and that therefore they must be and will
> be established. The statement of ideal is regarded as a suf-
> ficient guarantee of its ultimate realization.[5]

He then referred to Jones's *Christ's Alternative to Communism* as a prime example of "the most perfect swan song of liberal politics."[6]

Niebuhr held Jones in high regard and considered his book "a sincere and moving plea from one of the genuine saints of the missionary movement." Yet he dismissed Jones's view as demonstrating a "complete lack of relevance to the political and economic problems of the hour." Interestingly, Niebuhr used the following quote from Jones as an illustration of sentimental moralism: "the [human] mind . . . is becoming more and more latently Christian."[7]

It is debatable whether Niebuhr's critique of Jones was fair and justifiable. Regardless, it is hard to deny that Jones held an optimistic view of human nature, in particular of its latent propensity to convert to Christian faith. For instance, Jones was full of optimism about the future of Christianity in India when his very first book, *The Christ of the Indian Road*, was published in the mid-1920s:

> As the physical atmosphere becomes saturated with moisture and heavy to the point of precipitation so the spiritual atmosphere of India is becoming saturated with Christ's thoughts and ideals and is heavy to the point of precipitation into Christian forms and expression.
>
> We believe that India will fall intensely in love with the Christ of the Indian Road, that love will turn to glad submission to him as Saviour and Lord, that out of that loving submission will come a new radiant expression of him in thought and life.[8]

Some readers would have likely expected that Christianity would soon become a vital religious force in India, which almost a century later has not yet been realized.

When Jones described human nature, he agreed with Tertullian that the human soul is naturally Christian. Life without God is unnatural since it is an attempt to live against the nature of the human soul created for God. It is noteworthy that Jones regarded sin as unnatural—"an imposition, an intrusion," or "something for which we are not made." Sin can be compared to "sand in the eye" or "acid on a nerve"; "it causes inflammation, infection, and if not got rid of, then death."[9]

Jones did not specifically mention the name of Reinhold Niebuhr, but he made it clear that he was deliberately arguing against the theological trends of his time that were "prevailingly pessimistic."[10] He distinguished his understanding of sin from that of neoorthodoxy by preferring the term "estrangement" to "predicament" for describing human reality:

> The neo-orthodoxy uses the term "predicament" to describe [human] fallen state. I prefer "estrangement." Predicament depicts a person caught because of his sins. Estrangement depicts a person estranged from God, from himself, from life. Estrangement speaks of a relationship; predicament speaks of a condition—one centers your thought on God from whom you are estranged, and the other centers your thought on yourself, the predicament in which you find yourself.[11]

Jones must have been aware of the criticism that his view of human nature was overly optimistic. He made a point of stressing that he was not "teaching a rosy view of human nature which takes no account of [human] depravity and sin."[12] He did not hesitate to state that sin is "deeply, pervasively" in humans, and "has corrupted" humans.[13] However, even when Jones reflected on human depravity, he seldom grappled with or agonized over its seriousness. He rather quickly pointed to the unnaturalness of sin, and to the human need and potential for conversion: "'[Humankind] is made for conversion,' as the duck is made for the water, the bird is made for the air, the heart is made for love. . . . When you are converted and find Christ, you find yourself, your Homeland."[14]

Jones's inclination not to keep human sinfulness and divine grace in intense dialectic tension appears to be based on his commitment to the theological priority of God's transforming grace in Christ over the power of evil, which reflects the Wesleyan optimism of grace. In response to a question on whether his philosophy of life might not be too neat or rosy, he said, "I see evil, for no one can look into the face of Jesus Christ and not know what evil is. It killed him. But I gaze at him and glance at evil. If you glance at Jesus and gaze at evil, you cannot help being a pessimist. But if you gaze at Jesus and glance at evil, you cannot help being an optimist."[15]

Jones's optimistic view of human nature at times led him to be overly hopeful about the possibility of transforming individuals and societies, and it resulted in "a lack of social and political realism" in his scheme of social change.[16] Yet it was also instrumental in his willingness and eagerness to engage with people of different cultures and religions at the level of their deepest needs and aspirations, trusting that every encounter could hold the potential for conversion.

Conversion as Self-Surrender

It is noteworthy that Jones's own conversion experience profoundly shaped his perceptions of God and humanity as well as his theology and practice of evangelism. Looking back on his conversion, Jones noted, "Conversion was the pivot on which everything turned in my life"; it was as if "a tiny ray of light had pierced my darkness." With Christ, no longer the self, becoming the center of his being, the conversion experience brought him, *inter alia*, a sense of forgiveness and reconciliation and of wholeness and purpose, along with "a divine compulsion to share [God's grace] with everyone, everywhere."[17]

Jones was clearly aware that there is no standard type of conversion, since each is unique. Yet every genuine conversion involves all three aspects of human nature—intellect, emotion, and will—while "the center of conversion is the conversion of the will."[18] He described conversion as "a specific kind with a certain definite content and character leading to certain definite results in life."[19] It entails turning in "a new direction," acquiring "a new spirit" as the fruit of reconciliation with God and liberation from the guilt, and entering "a new sphere of living," that is, the Kingdom of God.[20] It was crucial for Jones that conversion be "set within the framework of the Kingdom of God,"[21] bringing the whole of life, individual and social, under the reality of God's reign.

Jones located the root of sin in the self, in the unsurrendered self. At the center of human disease is the self, and all else is symptom: "The problem is the same everywhere—the self, the self-centered self, the self-preoccupied self, the unsurrendered self. . . . I have only one remedy [which is self-surrender], for I find only one disease—self at the center, self trying to be God."[22] Since the unsurrendered self is the root of all evils, without self-surrender, Christians are paltering with the business of being Christians, and all efforts to deal with particular sins are only tinkering with symptoms.

People cling to and idolize things that are not primary and valued by God, among which are race (racism), nation (nationalism), religious community (ecclesiocentrism), class (classism), and material wealth (mammonism). Claiming absolute human allegiance, they become sources of false pride and illusory security. In order to enter the Kingdom of God, however, every person needs to surrender these human kingdoms. According to Jones, "the central citadel of all" is the kingdom of the self, the last thing that humans are willing to let go of and give up.[23]

Yet "the Christian faith in its New Testament form," stated Jones, "asks nothing less and nothing more than self-surrender to God." We as creatures are to surrender to God the Creator the self, "the one and only thing we own."[24] Thus, at the heart of conversion is the conversion of the self by self-surrender—the surrender of the center of one's life to Christ or a reorientation of life around Christ as the new center.

Jones stressed that religious education is not to be a substitute for conversion, since people "cannot know Christ by knowledge about Christ," but only "by surrender to and faith in and obedience to Him," that is, by conversion.[25] To be a Christian is none other than to belong to Christ by surrender and obedience to Him as Lord and Savior. Those sharing the gospel are then not to "be misled by a marginal need" of the person, but to be mindful that "the real crux is the surrender of the self."[26]

Jones provided a profound insight into the understanding of conversion as self-surrender by relating it to Jesus's crucifixion and God's character. On the cross, Jesus "aligned Himself with self-giving instead of self-saving. And in doing so He revealed the deepest thing in the heart of God—self-sacrifice."[27] In other words, Jesus's death on the cross, the ultimate archetype of self-surrender, revealed the essence of God's character: self-surrendering and self-giving love. Therefore, when God invites us to surrender ourselves, we are not asked to do what is strange to God but what is at the very heart of God and God's redemptive mission. "It only is the gospel," wrote Jones, "that dares say that God too suffers."[28]

Jones considered Revelation 7:17, which includes the phrase "the Lamb who is at the heart of the throne" (NJB), one of the most significant verses in the Bible. The Lamb was not simply slain on the cross but is at the center of the throne. For Jones, the implication was clear: God not only redeems through the cross but also rules from the cross by self-giving, self-sacrificial love. If the Lamb is at the heart of the throne, then self-surrender is not a marginal, occasional practice but "the deepest law of the universe."[29]

Conversion and Character

Integral to Jones's understanding of conversion is the formation and transformation of character. He was convinced that "the end and motive of Christianity, and therefore of Christian mission, is to produce Christ-like character."[30] Christian conversion entails the spiritual and moral renewal of one's very being evidenced by a change in character and life.

Jones sharply distinguished between conversion and proselytism, renouncing the latter. Proselytism is simply the exchange of one religion for another without involving any change in moral and spiritual character. He thus emphatically stated, "We . . . repudiate the idea of gaining mere numbers; we want character."[31] Writing on prose-lytism in the early 1930s, Jones criticized some missionary practices that drew people into Christianity without any qualification. The mere change of religion that does not involve "an inner change" in "every single department of life" is proselytism and not conversion:

> We will never be able to truly convert unless we get rid of proselytizing. We are not out for numbers . . . we are not out to dominate anyone's soul, we are not to impose something on others, we are not out to destroy everything in India's culture and past, but we are out to convert, first ourselves and then every [person] everywhere who is in spiritual and moral need. And that includes us all.[32]

For the formation and cultivation of character, Jones accorded a crucial place to discipline in his theology of conversion. Although discipline is the fruit, not the root, of conversion, they are inseparably interrelated:

> Salvation *is* by grace through faith in Christ, with nothing between. But—and this is the tragedy—in this discovery [during the Reformation] we threw away the necessity of discipline. . . . We cannot be saved by the discipline, but our salvation cannot be effective unless disciplined. There is really no clash between grace and discipline.[33]

The life of Jesus provides the best example of the faithful practice of spiritual disciplines: He read the Word by habit, prayed by habit, and proclaimed the good news by habit. "No converted person can live," stressed Jones, "without those habits at work vitally in his [or her] life": to be "scriptural," "prayerful," and "evangelistic."[34] On the walls of the Sat Tal Ashram was found: "This is a place of freedom through discipline."[35]

Character formation and holiness of life initiated by conversion are particularly crucial for evangelization in a post-Christendom society such as North America today. In this post-Christian era, people are suspicious of Christianity and search for evidences of the life of the gospel; they hunger for an authentic experience of the reality of God. The evidence of transformed character and life, through which the gospel becomes vital and visible, would make Christian witness credible and inviting.

Continuing Conversion

Regardless of the type of conversion experienced, every believer is in need of continuing conversion. A faithful Wesleyan, Jones wrote: Jesus "accepts me in my imperfections, but he doesn't leave me there. He holds me to perfection."[36] He often referred to himself as a Christian-in-the-making, one who is becoming Christlike in character, life, and witness. He reiterated, through his writings, the significance of continuing reformation for Christian life:

> Conversion [is] a once-and-for-all and yet an expanding experience to be applied to larger and larger areas of life.[37]
> That surrender is like being married. It is absolute—once and for all, but it is also unfolding. We say one complete and final "Yes," but many little "yes-es" come out of that big Yes.[38]

So there is a once-for-all surrender, and there is a continuous, day-by-day surrender. There is a growth in surrender. Self-surrender is a continuing principle as well as a once-for-all practice.[39] No Christian is fully Christianized. Our initial conversion is a limited surrender in which the change affects only certain areas of life. Conversion is thus to continue to grow deeper and broader so as to embrace the whole of life.

Jones captured the integral nature of conversion in these terms:

> Conversion is to Jesus Christ as a person and to the Kingdom of God as an order. . . . The nature of the Kingdom is

> social; the entrance into the Kingdom is personal by a new
> birth. You enter it personally; you live in it corporately.[40]

He stressed the need for conversion to extend to social life, overcoming sinful prejudices and exclusiveness based on race, religion, culture, economic class, and gender.

Serving as a missionary in India, Jones was viewed as "different from other missionaries in so far as he tried to relate the Gospel of Jesus Christ to the socio-political and cultural realities of the country."[41] A vocal critic of Western racially prejudiced social and international policies, he denounced the racism prevailing in the West as a great hindrance to the spread of the gospel in India. Reflecting on racism in the United States, he exclaimed: "A person is a 'person for whom Christ died.' We are all equal before God and therefore equal before [one another]"; "I was bound in every [person's] bondage. I could only be free in every [person's] freedom."[42]

Early in his faith journey, participating in class meetings, Jones grasped the significance of community for the unfolding conversion experience. He came to understand the communal nature of Christian faith, and he advocated the necessity of small groups for the nurture and care of souls. Christians need to be a part of a community that consists of those "who are under the process of redemption," a fellowship in which people are "unreservedly committed to Christ and unbreakably committed to each other."[43] Jones's transformative experience of the power of redemptive love in the class meeting later "became the idea and impulse back of the Christian Ashram movement."[44] Ashrams concretely demonstrated the communal nature of Christianity, crossing socioeconomic and national boundaries.

Conversion and Experience

Jones considered "the 'warmed heart' and the 'world parish'—experience and expression" as the two most distinguishing marks of Methodism.[45] He never tired of emphasizing the importance of experience in Christian conversion. If Jesus is the Word become flesh, He must become flesh in the heart and life of individual Christians; the Jesus of history has to become the Christ of experience. "My theology is based," asserted Jones, "not merely on the teachings of Christ but on the Person himself," who is a living, redemptive presence here and now.[46] He thus regretted that Mahatma Gandhi—whom he called one of the most Christlike persons in history—had "grasped the principles [of Jesus], but . . . missed the Person [of Jesus]." And he further regretted that it was "the cloud of racism enveloping the type of Christianity in South Africa" that kept Gandhi from having "a first-hand experience of Jesus," leading to his decision not to become a Christian.[47]

Not long after his own conversion, Jones came to learn an extremely valuable lesson, which would profoundly affect and shape his lifelong ministry as a missionary evangelist: Christ must be witnessed to and interpreted in terms of experience. His very first sermon, preached at his home church, was an absolute failure. He had to stop in the middle of delivery and to come down from the pulpit in shame and confusion:

> As I was about to leave the pulpit a Voice seemed to say to me, "Haven't I done anything for you?"
> "Yes," I replied, "You have done everything for me."
> "Well," answered the Voice, "couldn't you tell that?"
> "Yes, I suppose I could," I eagerly replied. So instead of going to my seat I came around in front of the pulpit below . . . and said: "Friends, I see I cannot preach, but I love Jesus Christ. . . . You know he has made life new for me, and though I cannot preach I am determined to love and serve him." At the close a lad came up and said, "Stanley, I wish I could find what you have found." He did find it then and there.

Jones came to realize that evening that he was called to be "not God's lawyer but his witness." He was not "to argue [God's] case for him" but to be in living communion with God, "so that there would always be something to pass on."[48]

His missionary experience in India corroborated his conviction that Christ must be interpreted in terms of experience. India wanted to know what Christians had found and what Christ had done for them, their personal religious experiences. Jones thus wrote, "We cannot merely talk about Christ to India—we must bring him. He must be a living vital reality—closer than breathing and nearer than hands and feet. We must be 'God-bearers.'"[49]

The Round Table conferences that Jones conducted were not focused on arguing over a doctrine or a sacred book, but they were deeply experiential. Richard Taylor, one of the early interpreters of Jones, thus observed, "Even now [in the 1970s] I know of nothing like this experience-based dialogue."[50] It was centered on concrete questions such as, "Where can we find God?" "What does religion produce in experience?" and "How can we live a spiritually vital life in which sin is overcome and character is renewed?" People of other religions wanted to learn about the Christ of experience, and Jones had to respond at the level of experience, sharing something real and vital. What Jones found was that the transforming effect of the experience-based dialogue was reciprocal. Participating in the Round Table Conferences, Christians themselves were renewed in their faith or even re-evangelized:

> We were compelled to rethink our problems in the light of the Non-Christian faiths and in the light of the religious experiences of non-Christians. So while these Conferences have been valuable in our approach to the Non-Christian faiths, they have proved of even greater value to us in facing our own problems spiritual and intellectual.[51]

For Jones, it was crucial that Christianity be authentically experienced by and expressed through each culture. He shared a profound missiological insight when he said that Christianity "must be particular before it can be universal" in order to be "a voice, not an echo." Thus, the Indian "must stand in the streams of India's culture and life and let the force of that stream go through his [or her] soul so that the expression of his [or her] Christianity will be essentially Eastern and not Western."[52] Jones was acutely aware that Jesus is "too great to be expressed by any one portion of humanity," and that "every nation has its peculiar contribution to make to the interpretation of Christianity."[53] Such conviction compelled him to present "the disentangled Christ—disentangled from being bound up with Western culture and Western forms of Christianity."[54]

Lessons for Today

Jones developed an integral and comprehensive understanding of conversion as self-surrender. His vision of conversion held together seemingly opposite elements in dialectic tension: free yet costly, once-and-for-all yet unfolding, personal and social, and individual as well as communal. He deeply believed in both the human need and potential for conversion and was unapologetic about his single-minded focus on conversion in ministry. Since the greatest human need is conversion, the church is not to reduce conversion to conversation or decision to dialogue. To be faithful to its calling, "the church will never sophisticate itself from [the] need of conversion."[55]

For Jones, conversion is not strange but natural to humans, as every person is created for conversion. Sin has perverted and depraved humans; however, the gospel is, in essence, the divine "Yes" to humanity, and Christ the divine "Yes" incarnated. Therefore "no one is farther than one step from God," that is, to "turn around in repentance and faith."[56] Evangelism is then not to be considered as "an alien intrusion into life" or "an unnatural demand."[57]

Jones emphasized that conversion is the regeneration of the old nature and not the transplantation of a new nature.[58] This view of conversion was echoed later by Andrew F. Walls, a Scottish Methodist missiologist: "[Conversion] is not about substituting something new for something old . . . it is turning what is already there; turning to Christ." Whether experienced as a definite crisis moment or as a gradual process, conversion is a radical reorientation of life that involves a "steady, relentless turning of all the mental and moral processes toward Christ."[59]

The church's evangelistic ministry does not stop when people are welcomed into the Christian faith and community. It must continue to invite and nurture them to be on a journey of redirecting their lives toward Christ. Since conversion is the turning of life in the direction of Christ, the church as evangelist needs to have an integral understanding of the life and teachings of Christ and "to be far more concrete in communicating the meaning of Christ's teachings for [its members'] life-context."[60] It is not to be abstract or vague about the nature and cost of Christian life and discipleship, being mindful of the two-thirds of those sitting in the pews who could still remain a field, not a force, for evangelism.

Jones's trust in God's transforming grace in Christ became the driving force behind his life as a relentless witness for Christ. It led him to devote himself, without reservation, to evangelism and to the transformation of the church and the world. For Jones, every moment and every encounter held the potential for conversion—of both himself and others—and his task as a missionary evangelist was to preach Christ with the assurance that "it is possible for anybody who is created in [God's] image to be re-created in that image."[61]

It is of paramount importance for the church today to recover an unwavering commitment to its evangelistic vocation. It must take to heart these words of warning from Jones: "When the church loses its power to convert, it loses its right to be called a church"; and unless it is transforming people's life in the likeness of Christ, "it is failing as a church of the living Christ."[62]

RETURNING TO THE ROUND TABLE

Mark R. Teasdale

There has been a pervasive sense of gloom spreading over churches in the United States during the early part of the twenty-first century, especially for mainline Protestant denominations and Roman Catholics. Once the reigning religious institutions, surveys of the American religious landscape have shown that many congregations are diminished, and the overall number of Christians in the United States is declining. At the same time, the number of people who claim no religious preference is climbing.[1]

However, this demographic shift is not as dire as it may seem. Additional research shows that even with the rise of people refusing to identify with a specific religion, there are a large number of people who are open to talking about spirituality. Indeed, there are more "unchurched" people open to having those discussions than there are Christians willing to speak to them.

According to LifeWay Research, 79 percent of people who are "unchurched," (meaning they have not attended a church service in more than six months outside of a special event such as a wedding or a holiday), are open to hearing a religious friend talk about his or her faith. Forty-seven percent said that they would not just listen but would engage in the conversation. Yet only 35 percent of the respondents said a Christian had ever discussed faith with them. Scott McConnell, executive director of LifeWay Research, summed up the findings by saying that many Christians avoid talking about their faith because they are afraid of offending their unchurched friends. Yet "unchurched Americans are not hostile to faith."[2]

The issue, then, is not whether Christians can evangelize in the new American landscape. It is clear that we not only can, but we will likely receive a good hearing if we do. The question is how to engage in conversations about the Christian faith that will be safe spaces for unchurched people to both share their views and to hear the gospel.

Well before the current demographic shifts in North America, E. Stanley Jones was facing a similar challenge in India. Confronted by a religiously plural culture consisting of Hindus, Buddhists, and Muslims, as well as a philosophical tradition that had already thought deeply about the nature and actions of God, he struggled to find a way to share the Christian faith. In *The Christ of the Indian Road*, Jones explained how his first step in overcoming this hurdle was to focus on sharing Jesus rather than getting bogged down with other messages:

> When I first went to India, I was trying to hold a very long line—a line that stretched clear from Genesis to Revelation, on to Western Civilization and to the Western Christian Church. I found myself bobbing up and down that line fighting behind Moses and David and Jesus and Paul and Western Civilization and the Christian Church. I was worried. There was no well-defined issue. . . . I had the ill-defined but distinctive feeling that the heart of the matter was being left out. Then I saw that I could, and should, shorten my line, that I could take my stand at Christ and . . . refuse to know anything save Jesus Christ and him crucified. . . . I saw that the gospel lies in the person of Jesus, that he himself is the Good News, that my one task was to live and to present him.[3]

This focus on Christ as the sole message was essential. However, Jones still needed to discover the process by which he would share Christ in a culture with such deep existing beliefs about God. The traditional meetings that missionaries held, in which they gave lectures and fielded questions, were not sufficient vehicles to deliver this message.

Jones found the answer in the Round Table Conferences, intimate gatherings of approximately thirty people who were committed to listening and speaking about their religious experiences. These conferences proved very effective for Jones in India, and they also have promise for teaching us to engage in meaningful conversations with unchurched neighbors today.

The First Round Table

Jones relayed the history of Round Table Conferences in his book, *Christ at the Round Table*. He described how he was holding a meeting in which an attendee said to him, "I hear you speak about finding Christ. What do you mean by it?" Jones understood that this was a sincere question and that it demanded something other than an academic answer. His interlocutor "wanted to know about this Christ of experience."[4] So Jones shared his personal story of how he had come to place his faith in Jesus Christ. Then Jones shared how those in attendance could find Christ for themselves.

After this experience, Jones exclaimed, "Our eyes were opened to the possibilities in the small selected group."[5] He found that having a small group of people share about their personal faith was a powerful tool for evangelism, allowing for give-and-take conversation on a deeper level than traditional meetings did.

Fresh from this discovery, Jones was holding a series of meetings in another town and discussed with a local church official what had happened in the previous meeting. The official recommended that they try a similar approach with a selected group of local men. Jones agreed. When the group gathered, Jones opened the meeting by inviting each attendee to share "what religion was meaning to them *in experience.*" It went "amazingly," so Jones went on to make Round Table Conferences a hallmark method of his ministry in India.[6]

Rules for the Round Table

As he developed the Round Table Conferences, Jones established rules for participating. First, he limited the conferences to no more than thirty people, who were carefully selected and invited. He did this to ensure that everyone in attendance would have an opportunity to speak and that the people speaking would be respectful of one another.

The participants were called to speak out of their experiences only. Jones wanted to bypass the intellectual arguments that often arose when discussing "religious concepts."[7] He was not interested in hammering out clarity around doctrine or proving the historical accuracy of specific events. He wanted people to talk about the actual effect that religion had on their lives. As Jones described it, "As we face the problems of life . . . what has religion brought to us? What has it brought us of light, of moral dynamic for personal and social life, of inward peace and harmony, of redemption from sin and from the power of this world, of God?"[8]

Given the personal nature of the sharing, he also encouraged people to speak candidly about what they believed. He did not want them "to reduce everything to a least common denominator." Rather, "if a religion centers for them in Rama, or Krishna, or Buddha, or the Vedanta, or the Koran, or Christ, to say so."[9] Those who had "dismissed God" from their lives were equally welcome to share. So long as each person spoke out of his sincere beliefs, and listened to the others, he was welcome to share whatever he brought to the table.[10]

To avoid anyone dominating the discussion, wordiness was also discouraged. Jones was fond of using a story about a Hindu swami seeking for God, who would abruptly leave if a person speaking to him about God went on for too long. The swami "knew that [the person he was listening to] had not found [God], for if he had, he could have said so clearly, and could have put his finger upon its meaning for life."[11]

William M. Pickard Jr., a missionary who became general secretary of a mission organization that Jones founded, admonishes us not to think that the conferences were facile sharing about personal faith on a surface level. For Jones, a person's religion was worthwhile only insofar as it guided and blessed that person's life. This kind of speaking about religion was a quest for reality.[12]

To determine the lived reality of a religion, Jones rallied the scientific method to his cause. Rather than relying on traditional methods of comparing religious beliefs or challenging the logic of specific doctrines, he wanted people around the table to share the results of their personal religious experimentation. As he put it:

> As we sit around in a circle . . . we suggest that we have had the controversial, the comparative, and the dogmatic approaches to religion. There is another possible approach. Let us come at it by the method more closely akin to the scientific method—a method so gripping to the mind of the world today. This method has three outstanding things in it: Experimentation, Verification, and Sharing of Results. I suggest to them that we try this method. We are all religious men, some more and some less, and we have all been experimenting with this matter of religion over a number of years. We have tried it as a working hypothesis of life. . . . What have we and what are we verifying as true in experience? Will you share with us the results of your verification?[13]

By appealing to the scientific method as an objective means for approaching religion, Jones was able to disarm people who entered the conference ready to battle for the supremacy of their religion or their specific version of their religion. As Pickard put it, "In the Round Table Conference there was no pitting of one religion against another.

There was only witness to what one's own religious faith has done and is doing in life."[14]

As Pickard observed, "This is dialogue at its best—and evangelism at its best."[15] By leveling the playing field so that all people could share their religious experiences, Jones avoided the traditional difficulty of the evangelist being the chief speaker who people must choose to either accept or reject. Instead, he created an atmosphere in which the Christian voice could speak equally with other voices. While some might worry that this equity would devalue the gospel, making it just one more idea among many, it did just the opposite. By adopting a listening position, the Christian embodies the love of Jesus who emptied Himself that He might become human (Phil. 2:7). People are more willing to receive the evangelist's message, because the evangelist does not act as spiritual superior—something that evangelists have too often done—but is willing to treat others as Jesus did.

Lessons for Today

This approach to evangelism fits well in the American context today for three reasons. First, its humility would be welcomed by those who are willing to engage in dialogue about the gospel. While LifeWay's research shows there is openness to these conversations, that research comes on the heels of warnings that many people also have preconceived negative opinions about the church and institutional Christianity. The Barna Institute completed a three-year study in 2007 in which they found that "among young non-Christians, nine out of the top 12 perceptions [of Christianity] were negative. Common negative perceptions include that present-day Christianity is judgmental (87%), hypocritical (85%), old-fashioned (78%), and too involved in politics (75%)."[16]

Given that these negative views focus heavily on how closed-minded Christians are perceived to be toward other groups, the Round Table Conference model would be a breath of fresh air to many unchurched Americans. It would signal that we are not setting ourselves in a position to judge others, but are coming in a humble posture to listen, learn, and share. We would not appear to press people to accept specific truths, but we would be gesturing to the truth that we experience in our own lives.

Second, the Round Table Conference is practicable even if Christianity is a minority religion. Christians made up a tiny percentage of the Indian population when Jones evangelized there, as they still do at the beginning of the twenty-first century (approximately 2.3% of the population).[17] Moreover, Hinduism and Buddhism, the two most prominent religions, existed well before the life of Jesus Christ. As powerful as the gospel is, there was no cultural mandate for Indians to pay attention to it. There was no reason that Christians should have had a place at the Indian table.

To enter such a situation in anything other than a quiet and listening posture would have been absurd. Christians needed to respect the Indians' existing beliefs, not as mistaken attempts to reach the truth of the gospel, but as deep reflections about God made by serious and devout people. Only if Christians could be good students of what gave meaning to other peoples' lives could they hope to earn a seat at the table. As Douglas Ruffle, a longtime missionary who reflected on the work of E. Stanley Jones, put it, "Jones learned the importance of listening to others and practicing authentic openness to others' beliefs."[18]

The Round Table Conferences allowed Christians to engage in this kind of listening, but they also made room for the Christians to speak. By setting up the conferences so that all people could share based on their experiences, Jones found a structure that did not challenge the majority status of Hinduism or Buddhism, while equalizing everyone's sharing. Hindus and Buddhists were able to share fully about their religious experiences, unconstrained by any ground rules about what sorts of ideas or beliefs they presented. At the same time, the minority status of the Christian was effectively removed, since Christians could equally share about their experiences with Christ.

This was a masterful move by Jones, and it is one that we should learn from as we evangelize in the United States today. While Christians are far from the minority religious group in the United States in the early twenty-first century, and will remain the dominant religion for many decades to come—even with the steady decline in the mainline Protestant and Catholic churches—Americans now see the church as a less important institution. LifeWay found in 2014 that 55 percent of Americans described the church as "declining" and 42 percent as "dying."[19]

In such a setting Christians would do well to approach people with the same openness that Jones exemplified, recognizing that we come from a position of cultural weakness. Entering into a dialogue about what has brought meaning to people's lives with the promise that we will "suspend any tendency to evaluate or judge and, instead, listen,"[20] frees us to speak on equal terms without threatening the cultural and social strength of others' meaning-making structures.

Third, dialogue helps Christians articulate their faith. As Jones confessed, "I never approach these Round Tables without feeling my heart beat a little faster."[21] He knew he was bringing the gospel, but only as one presenter among many intelligent, committed people. He wondered, "Would our gospel ring true to reality? . . . Was our gospel a broken light from God, illuminating patches and portions of life but leaving life as a whole unilluminated? Or was it God's adequate answer to man's need—intellectual, moral, spiritual, social?"[22] Struggling with this question, he exclaimed, "I had been forced to come to grips with the big, relevant issues of life in contact with other faiths and other ways of life."[23]

Some Christians were skeptical of Jones's approach. They worried that his openness to other religions would undercut his commitment to the Christian faith, especially when his experiences at the Round Table Conferences led him to attend spiritual retreats led by Gandhi. Yet they found that Jones's insistence on pursuing the truth of a meaningful experience of life actually drew him closer to the gospel.

As one friend wrote to him, "I was afraid you would not come out *a missionary*. But you *have*."[24]

More than just clarify his thinking, Jones found that his faith grew to the point that he could recognize and welcome the goodness of God in other people and their beliefs, whether or not they were Christian. Drawing from Paul's teaching in 1 Corinthians 3:21-23,[25] Jones argued that the Round Table Conferences teach Christians both liberty and law. They have liberty to claim all good things that God offers. However, they can do this only so long as they remain in Christ; that is the law. So, Jones explains, "All great religious teachers are yours. Here the gospel offers intellectual and spiritual liberty. Provided we remember whose we are, we are free to take from all religious teachers whatever of light and truth they have discovered and realized."[26]

Thus, Jones found that his faith grew because of the Round Table Conferences. They sharpened his eyes to see where God was visible in the experiences of others, and he celebrated the situations in which he found God. Far from drawing him away from believing in Jesus Christ as the center of human faith, he drew closer to Christ, who made it possible for him to recognize, receive, and celebrate all this goodness. Hence, Jones could have a deep personal respect for Gandhi (who he referred to as "the saint and patriot of India" and a "great soul"), even sitting at his feet to learn from him,[27] and at the same time plead with Gandhi to accept Christ.[28]

Jones went so far as to claim that having this view of Christ made people more effective in sharing the gospel. He observed, "There are those who in order to be more universal tone down the distinctively Christian things. But you cannot be more universal by being less Christian. In the Round Tables those who struck the deepest Christian notes made the more universal appeal."[29]

Additionally, Jones believed the Round Table Conferences clarified the purpose of Christian mission. He wrote: "As the missions sit at the Round Table let them fearlessly go over their motives and aims and spirit and let them courageously eliminate everything that does not fit in with the mind of Christ. In that direction lies the future."[30] For Jones, missions had too long been caught up in holding "the long line" he described himself once trying to defend. Many of these principles were impediments to missionary work, especially the church's relationship to imperialism.[31] By sitting at the Round Table Conferences, missionaries could pare away these burdens and offer their unalloyed experience of Christ.

Jones and his fellow missionaries took these lessons and developed their "evangelistic objective" as "the production of Christ-like character, through faith in and fellowship with Christ the living Saviour, and through corporate sharing of life in a divine society."[32] In doing so, they sidestepped the political and cultural snares of trying to plant a church or preach a gospel that was dominated by Western values.

Today, American mainline Protestants and Roman Catholics are unprepared to articulate their faith, and consequently these churches have lost their public witness. Kenda Creasy Dean, exploring why so many teenage Christians in the United States have lukewarm faith, credits the phenomenon in part to adults in the church. Parents and mentors have never taught adolescents how to talk about their faith or helped them learn the concepts and vocabulary to explain what Christians believe and how faith informs daily life.[33] As a result youth and young adult Christians are theologically and biblically illiterate.

Certainly, Christians should first learn and practice speaking about our faith within the church.[34] However, speaking about our faith within the church, according to Jones, is insufficient. It never forces us to ask the deep questions or face the uncertainties that we derive from sharing our faith in dialogue with people who hold alternative beliefs. Our faith grows weak because we are never pushed to consider our beliefs from another perspective or exposed to the goodness of God that Christ makes available in the experiences of others. Isolation limits our capacity to engage in evangelism.

Jones did not shy from evangelistic witness in a pluralistic world.

After describing how Gandhi had turned away from the Christian faith on the edge of conversion, because of a "worldly, dull, and drowsy" congregation, Jones opined: "A great deal of the irreligion and lack of interest in things spiritual can be laid down to the smugness, the complacency, the lack of a radiant God-consciousness and the dying out in the churches of the spirit of adventure in following Jesus."[35] The Round Table Conferences invite us into that adventure.

Setting up a Round Table in the Church

Jones considered the usefulness of Round Table Conferences within the church as well as outside it. As it is today, the church of Jones' time was rent with factionalism and distrust. Chief among these were the doctrinal battles between the Fundamentalists and the Modernists. As deeply ensconced as people were in their respective positions within the church, Jones believed that Round Table Conferences might bring healing and unity. He first discovered this possibility when he had the opportunity to sit at the Round Table Conferences in India with Christians from a variety of denominational and theological perspectives. He explained:

> We might have gathered from the ends of the earth . . . from many nations and denominations, with no previous intimation of what we were going to be called on to do, so there could be no possibility of fitting in statement with statement, yet the moment we dropped to the level of Christian experience, we were talking the same language.[36]

Applying the logic, that the Round Table Conferences called Christians to a higher plane of discussion in which they verified their lived experiences of Jesus Christ rather than debated denominational dogmas, Jones went on suggest a way forward in the Fundamentalist/ Modernist controversy. Those who experienced Christ deeply were just as able to use Paul's logic in 1 Corinthians 3 to claim the good in each of the two camps as they were to claim the good in other religions. Jones is worth quoting at some length here:

> I wonder if this attitude of Paul toward the other great religious teachers would not help us in the situation within the border of the Christian Church at the present time. Evidently, Paul and Apollos and Cephas differed sufficiently in their interpretations of the gospel to produce groups in Corinth to whom the respective interpretations appealed. They were in danger of being permanently divided because of this fact, when Paul arrested the process of disintegration by showing them that at the center, Christ, they were one; they were wrong in centering their life in the differing interpretations rather than in the Interpreted Christ.[37]

Accordingly, Jones stated that, rather than be claimed by the Fundamentalist or Modernist camp, he could hear the good things that each assented to and could agree to those things in the name of Christ. Jones did not belong to the Fundamentalists or the Modernists; but in Christ, both the Fundamentalists and the Modernists belonged to *him*.[38] "And," he concluded, "that remembrance of possession by Christ is the inward standard by which the chaff can be separated from the wheat. His mind is the final but unfolding standard by which all things must be judged."[39]

Jones offered this challenge to the church in the 1920s; and it is a challenge that he leaves for us today. In a time when mainline Protestants and Roman Catholics are wracked by cultural pressures and doctrinal debate, Jones calls us to the Round Table to hear one another speak of our experiences of Jesus Christ. What is the hypothesis about Him we have used to make sense of our lives? What verification have we experienced to show our hypothesis to be right or wrong? On this level of experience we may be able to make headway where we have too often been driven back by the strong tides of dogmatic, unreflective, intellectual beliefs.

Jones gives two caveats as we approach this Round Table within

RETURNING TO THE ROUND TABLE ■

the church. One, we must remember that it is possible to be deceived by our own experiences. For this reason, he reminds us that "the place of final certainty and authority is at the junction where the Jesus of history becomes the Christ of experience, and where the resultant individual experience is corroborated and corrected by the collective experience."[40] It is not enough for us to experience something. We need to bring our experiences with Christ into conversation with the scriptural witness and the corporate witness of the church throughout time, and be corrected by these witnesses if necessary.

Two, we need a real experience of Christ. Jones tells us that there are two types of conversion. There is a horizontal conversion in which a person may "change from one religion to another, leaving the person on the same level of character and life."[41] What God desires for us, and what the Christian should seek, is a vertical conversion in which "a spiritual change is wrought by Christ that lifts us from sin to goodness, from discord to harmony, from selfishness to sacrifice, from ourselves to God, and gives us a new sphere of living, the Kingdom of God."[42] Jones repeatedly describes Christians who, because of their conversion, so radiated the joy and peace of Christ that other people could not help but recognize the power of Jesus Christ in them.

The Round Table Conferences are a powerful tool for bringing unity within the church and evangelizing our unchurched neighbors. However, they remain powerful only if those who participate in them are faithful to the full Christian faith of the Scripture and the church, and only if we ourselves have experienced the transforming power of Jesus Christ. We must start with Jesus first, and then we can discover the gift of the Round Table.

THE CHRISTIAN ASHRAM

Thomas R. Albin

Of all the notes that make up my *Song of Ascents*, one of
the most important is the Ashram note. Without it I would
have lacked a disciplined fellowship . . . [where I could]
live out my life in a close-knit fellowship of the Spirit—they
responsible to me and I responsible to them, at a very deep
level, the level of experimental living . . . their transformations have been an invitation and a spur to further transformations in me. They have helped make me.[1]

In the final decade of his life, E. Stanley Jones wrote the passage
in the above epigraph. The Christian Ashram was and is the most
enduring source of the evangelistic ministry of E. Stanley Jones. It is
unique. No other Christian missionary or evangelist in the Protestant
tradition has so intentionally rooted and grounded his or her ministry in
the power of Jesus Christ incarnate in the life of the community. Jones's
words are a lived reality in the movement begun in India in 1930 and in
North America in 1940.

This chapter will provide a brief overview of "a close-knit fellowship of the Spirit . . . at a very deep level" that was able to spur

"further transformations" in Jones's life and message—and in turn, transform the hearts and lives of others in pluralistic societies around the world. The fact that today, more than thirty Christian Ashrams continue to bear spiritual fruit in many different countries around the world is a validation of this ongoing evangelistic *missio Dei* (mission of God)—in Christ—reconciling the world to Himself.

The Context of the Ashram in India

The Methodist Board of Mission sent Jones to India in 1907. He learned to love the people and appreciate their culture—the first steps for any authentic proclamation of the good news in a pluralistic culture. Jones gradually learned the value of the ancient Indian practice of *ashram*: to go away from hard work to sit at the feet of a guru to learn important truths. In ancient Sanskrit, *a* means "away from" and *shram* means "hard work." So *ashram* literally means "away from hard work," or a place of retreat and rest. In India, ashrams are normally held in a place where the beauty of nature provides a context for greater spiritual insight, "where in simplicity and disciplined corporate living the 'chelas,' or disciples, would seek for 'moksha,' or salvation."[2] Each ashram had a "guru," which literally means a dispeller of darkness, a teacher who provides spiritual enlightenment to those who came to learn.

Jones slowly discerned the value of the ashram as an authentic and indigenous means to bring the truth of Jesus Christ to the people. It would be a Christian Ashram where Jesus Christ, the Word become flesh and the Light of the world, would be the guru, teacher, and dispeller of darkness. In his book, *Along the Indian Road,* Jones describes his perspective on the missional context in India:

> The Indian spirit is difficult to define, but anyone who has come in contact with it knows what I mean – an inner poise, a spiritual sensitiveness, and a love of simplicity, an emphasis on the gentler virtues, a spirit of devotion, and an ascetic tinge. Just the spirit to be touched and redeemed by the Christ spirit. The adventure of putting them together

was a glorious one and I believe that the Ashram was a magnificent vehicle.[3]

The Origin and Culture of the Christian Ashram

In 1930 the Ashram that Jones founded at Sat Tal was a forest school for meditation and prayer, designed to "produce a type of Christianity more in touch with the soul of India."[4] He described the missionary principle and evangelistic practice of the Christian Ashram in agricultural terms:

> Some people would surmise because we have a Hindu term that therefore the Christian Ashram is an amalgamation between Christianity and Hinduism. Nothing could be further from the reality. Eclecticisms pick and choose, syncretisms combine, but only life assimilates. The Christian faith, being life, assimilates. Like the plant which reaches into the soil and picks out things akin to its own nature, takes them up into the purpose of its life, but transforms them according to the laws of its own being, so the Christian faith reaches into the culture of every nation and takes out things which can be assimilated into its purpose, but in so doing so makes something entirely different.[5]

Jones knew that Hindus, Buddhists, Sikhs, Jains, Jews, Muslims, agnostics, and atheists can agree that Jesus is a person to be honored and emulated. His theology of prevenient grace, and his growing certainty of the universal appeal of the Word become flesh in the person of Jesus Christ, helped him realize there was no need to diminish any other faith tradition. People did not have to be Christian to admire Jesus. They needed a place where everyone was welcome to come and experience Jesus—to live and learn from the people who did follow Him. Therefore, the culture and customs of the Christian Ashram were to reflect the teachings of Jesus. The mission of the Christian Ashram was to be "the Kingdom of God in miniature":

> But the center of that Center is the Word become flesh.
> Philosophies and religions are the Word become word, a
> philosophy or a moralism. In Jesus the Word has become
> flesh. If so, then the center of our manifestation of that
> Word become flesh must be that this Word must become
> flesh in us. If Christianity is looked on as a teaching—a
> philosophy or a moralism—then the group will become a
> discussion group where we get verbal answers to verbal
> questions. If the emphasis is on the Word become flesh,
> then the group must not find an answer, but be the answer
> in their corporate life. They must be the Word of the King-
> dom become flesh—a Kingdom in miniature.[6]

From the beginning, the Christian Ashram was intended to reflect
the Kingdom of God that Jesus came to announce and establish. In
this Kingdom the barriers that separate and divide people were to be
overcome:

> Imperfectly, of course, because made up of imperfect peo-
> ple, but in some real way the new order realized; univer-
> salize that, and you have the answer. . . . If the group is to
> be the Kingdom, then we must get down barriers, for the
> Kingdom is God's redemptive invasion of us. So we get
> down the barriers of race and class. The Kingdom is color-
> blind and class-blind; it sees a person as a person for whom
> Christ died. . . . Then we get down the barriers that titles
> bring. Those who have titles are high caste, and those who
> don't are low caste. So we leave all titles at the door. There
> are no more bishops, professors, doctors, judges—there is
> simply "Brother Stanley" or "Sister Premi." This has a psy-
> chological leveling effect, for it's not easy to be high and
> mighty if someone is calling you by your first name. We add
> the "Brother" and the "Sister," for it is a family of God.[7]

Even more specific to the Indian context was the cultural division of labor and worth created by the caste system. To embody the
Kingdom where Jesus is Lord, Jones knew that there had to be an
intentional practice that embodied a different social order. He wrote:

We get down the barriers between those who work with their hands and those who do not. Those who do not work with their hands are supposedly high caste, and those who do are supposedly low caste. So we get down that barrier by having a Work Period each day, when everybody works with his or her hands. We harness our exercise period to constructive tasks; we leave the place better than we found it.[8]

Jones believed in and followed Jesus as Lord. Since Jesus washed feet and served, Jones did the same. In fact, he enjoyed seeing the laboring classes lifted to a new level of dignity while he, as the honored leader from the United States, took on the role of a "sweeper" (one who cleaned toilets) and a trash collector.

The Full-Time and Part-Time Ashram

The Indian ashram was understood as a year-round place of pilgrimage and learning. The beginning of the Christian Ashram was "a two-month, part-time Ashram during the vacation period, May and June, the hottest season of the year. Missionaries, British officials, and Indians would join us and have a 'vacation with God.'"[9] The fact that participants held very different views about religion, politics, and economics was not a problem. All were welcome, all were treated with respect, and diversity was valued. It was in this context that Jones learned something important for his ongoing work as an evangelist actively engaged in the work of spiritual and social transformation:

One of the first lessons we learned was that the human mind breaks up between conservative and radical. Never once through those years did the discussion break up between the Westerners and Easterners. It was always between radical and conservative—the radical Indian and the radical Westerner on one side and the conservative Indian and the conservative Westerner on the other. That is a good division: if we were all conservative, we would dry up;

and if we were all radical, we would bust up! But between the pull back of the conservative and the pull ahead of the radical we make progress in a middle direction.[10]

The evangelistic mission of the Christian Ashram in India was not a story of easy progress or continual success. For example, Jones initially dreamed of a full-time Christian Ashram in Lucknow where he lived, similar to the ashrams of Gandhi and Tagore. Instead, it failed after several years. In Jones's own words:

The disbanding of the Ashram as a full-time Ashram, while it seemed a calamity at the time, led to a new form. It was transferred to America in 1940 as a part-time Ashram. As a part-time Ashram it has spread throughout the world. . . . As a full-time Ashram it could not have been transferred to another social climate; as a part-time Ashram of about a week in length it has proved that it could be transferred—and universalized. So the calamity became opportunity.[11]

In the years after Jones's death, the summer Ashram in Sat Tal adapted to the changes of the culture. Instead of two full months in the summer, it takes place over two weeks every year—in English—from May 15 to May 29, followed by a second, two-week Ashram conducted in Hindi from June 1 to 14. In North America, Japan, Korea, and Scandinavia, a typical Christian Ashram takes place over three to six days.[12]

Key Elements of the Christian Ashram

The Christian Ashram experience begins with a time of welcome and orientation followed by an opportunity for voluntary self-disclosure known as the Open Heart. Guided by the evangelist, participants answer three questions: 1) Why are you here? 2) What do you want? 3) What do you need from God before this event is over? According to Jones:

> The last question is the really important one. . . . We has-
> ten to say that you don't have to tell your needs, and you'll
> not be out of the fellowship if you don't tell your needs;
> but you'll be poorer, and we'll be poorer if you don't . . .
> people, from forty to four hundred in number, coming to-
> gether from all walks of life and from all denominations
> and all ages, for the first time in the first few hours tell their
> needs straight off, without any maneuvering or urging . . .
> they will—everywhere around the world . . . provided the
> leader begins by telling his own needs. I do. It is a catharsis.
> To bring up your needs and look at them fairly and honestly
> is halfway to the solution.[13]

The Open Heart is invaluable for evangelism in a pluralistic society. It provides insight into the spiritual needs of the participants, allowing the evangelist and Bible teacher to focus their teaching and preaching to meet the expressed needs of the community.

At the conclusion of the Christian Ashram is the Overflowing Heart. Participants express gratitude for the work God has done in their hearts. This is a spiritual opportunity

> to do what one of the lepers did when, having been healed,
> he turned back and fell at the feet of Jesus and said: "Thank
> you, thank you." That is psychologically as well as spiritu-
> ally sound. It is a law of the mind that that which is not
> expressed dies. Impression minus expression equals depres-
> sion. To express it is to impress it. It is also spiritually sound.
> It attaches the changed person to Jesus Christ and not to
> the movement through which the change came.[14]

Immediately after the Open Heart, and concluding just before the Overflowing Heart, the entire Christian Ashram is undergirded with prayer. Participants and leaders make a commitment to pray in thirty- or sixty-minute shifts, twenty-four hours a day, for the entire Ashram.

Each full day of a typical Christian Ashram would include time for 1) the "morning watch or devotion"; 2) Bible study; 3) a presentation of the "church in action," led by someone who had enriched the life of his or her local congregation with insights gained in a previous Ashram; 4) the Work Hour; 5) the Evangelist Hour; 6) the "Ashram Graces" sung before and after each meal; 7) the Family Meeting immediately after lunch; 8) an extended afternoon break to allow time for rest, recreation, special interest discussions, or activities; and 9) Prayer and Reflection Groups.

At the conclusion of an Ashram there may be a Talent Time during which participants can share their special gifts. There is always a Healing Service, a Communion Service, and the installation of the local volunteer board of directors called The Twelve.[15] The final event before the group departs is called the Closing Circle. Participants join hands and form a large circle as a physical reminder that everyone is valued, included, and blessed, using "these words written on the wall of the Sat Tal Ashram: 'Unreservedly given to God, unbreakably given to each other.' The fellowship is an unbreakable fellowship, for it is in Christ and not in that particular session. That breaks up. He abides."[16] Then the evangelist says, "Jesus is Lord," and the people respond with their final affirmation, "Jesus is Lord!"

The Leadership Structure

In 1950 the first Christian Ashram in Canada was organized under the sponsorship of the Canadian Council of Churches. In 1951 the Federal Council of Churches in the United States of America was renamed the National Council of Churches. While the ecumenical mission and theological credibility of the Christian Ashram in North America benefited greatly from these two church bodies, it also constrained the mission. Local leaders were told what to do and when to do it. All evangelists were decided by the Council staff. There was no possibility for developing local leadership.

Jones could see that the top-down approach of the Department of Evangelism (National Council of Churches) was hindering the growth and vitality of the movement: "The current situation is static and does not give room for spontaneous development and little room for the guidance of the Holy Spirit."[17] So in December 17, 1957, in Travis County, Texas, the American Christian Ashrams was incorporated. In 1961 the name was officially changed to the United Christian Ashrams. From the incorporation of the new missional structure in 1957, until the death of its founder on January 25, 1973, the movement grew rapidly in the USA and Canada, as well as around the world, reaching more people in more places for Christ.

The new structure empowered new leaders to adapt the "one-week camp or retreat" model and experiment with one-day and weekend Christian Ashrams in local churches.[18]

Lessons for Today

There are a few things we can learn for today from Jones. First, the idea of a God retreat is critical. The need to get away and experience God in a new way is something we all need. Ashrams are one model for doing spiritual renewal in a structured way. Second, we need to practice not getting stuck on roles. It is easy to fall into a trap of being served when in a role as leader, but the Ashram helps us to reclaim a focus on what it means to lead like Jesus. Third, the work of introspection is critical. The questions that frame an Ashram help one to look deep inside so that he or she can, in fact, become more open to others. It is when we develop a sense of who we are that we can be open to others and celebrate who they are.

A fourth lesson is of particular interest to Western Christians: the Western church is an incomplete expression of the reign of God that must be in dialogue with the global church. The goal was not just reconciling individual Indians to God through Christ; Jones was also reconciling the whole Western missionary enterprise to non-Western expressions of Christianity. By persuading Western Christians that they could learn from Asian, and later, African Christians, he reconciled the Western church to a richer and deeper experience of the Kingdom of

God and to a more complete and more responsible commitment to Kingdom purposes throughout the world.[19]

Christian Ashrams help us become open to receiving from others so that we can be transformed.

Conclusion

This movement, born in the heart of India and nurtured in the heart of Jones, has universal congruence with the mission of God. The Christian Ashram was and is a place where "home" is experienced here and now—the Kingdom of God in miniature—and where things done on earth are a foretaste of heaven.

Jones left behind a "close-knit fellowship of the Spirit—they responsible to me and I responsible to them, at a very deep level, the level of experimental living."[20] He had achieved his primary desire: the Christian Ashram remained an "organism" and had not become a rigid "organization." Jones acknowledged the need for structure, and he provided it. However, he constantly pointed to the universality of Christ and the infinite creativity of the Holy Spirit:

> It is my earnest desire that the Ashram movement be kept open theologically, spiritually and practically as for my whole life I have attempted to be; evangelical and evangelistic, in the sense of being responsive to and obedient to the whole Gospel, commending it to all mankind; ecumenical, transcending all denominational and sectarian division; inclusive, . . . perpetually relevant to the times and the real needs of humankind; committed to Christ and his Kingdom; . . . guided by the Holy Spirit, together with the combined wisdom of the concerned and committed fellowship.[21]

The impact of the Christian Ashram on Jones himself has been clearly demonstrated. The story of the expansion of the movement inside India and around the world is a living testament to the power of the Holy Spirit and the enduring value of this evangelistic method.

At its best, every person attending the Christian Ashram is welcomed and valued as a child of God. This message was incarnate in Jesus Christ, the Word become flesh, and now embodied in a community. People of any faith or no faith are welcomed to come and experience "the Kingdom of God in miniature" where Jesus is Lord.

The Christian Ashram was a life-giving immersion in the Christian Way. Everything demonstrated and practiced at the Ashram could be continued at home in a daily, personal Ashram or in the local church.

Today, the need remains for a life-affirming, warmhearted, intellectually honest, theologically informed, Christ-centered, non-anxious, joyful, self-surrendered, and Spirit-empowered way to live. This can be described in a sermon; but it can be demonstrated only in a living community.

LEADING CHANGE IN A PLURAL WORLD

THE ART OF CHRISTIAN ADVOCACY AND ORCHESTRATION

Brian Yeich

Throughout our history, Christians have asked: How ought we address systemic, public issues that confront our society and church? Especially given the highly charged public sphere of the present time, how do we engage those issues in a way that is faithful to the gospel and avoids doing harm? How are Christians to engage those in leadership in the local, regional, national, and even international spheres? How are we to be change agents in such a time as this? By any stretch of the imagination we live in uncertain times; but as Ellsworth Kalas has said, "In every age there have been uncertain times and challenges that seemed to be apocalyptic in proportion."[1]

As mentioned earlier in this book, E. Stanley Jones was known, not only as a missionary, evangelist, and theologian, but also as a respected international leader. While he never held political office, his influence was felt at the highest levels of international discourse and policy making, even though his influence on the cultural and political ideas of the early and mid-twentieth century has largely been forgotten by cultural and even ecclesial leaders. Yet Jones left a leadership legacy we should not soon forget, especially in terms of his willingness to engage those with power and influence.

Jones lived through some of the most tumultuous times in history, including two world wars, the Korean War, the Vietnam War, assassinations of major world leaders, and the rise of Communism. Yet despite what, on several occasions, might have seemed as the end of civilization, Jones maintained an optimism and hope grounded in his faith in Jesus Christ and his unshakable belief in the Kingdom of God. So how should we Christians respond to those in power? Perhaps the life and work of Jones can provide a template for Christian witness.

Let us consider two helpful viewpoints for looking at the work of Jones and his influence on those in power: First, advocacy; and second, what Daniel Batson refers to as the "orchestration of prosocial motives."[2] Defining these terms briefly will help us explore how Jones went about encouraging those in power to make positive change.

Rob Davis defines *advocacy* as

> a planned, intentional process of exploring, naming and challenging injustices (the failure, intentional or not, to use power appropriately) embedded in human structures (formal or informal) that constrain human flourishing with the goal of bringing about changes that will enable that flourishing.[3]

This work is neither haphazard nor random but involves planning and intention. It stems from the recognition of injustices, especially those arising out of systems and structures that contribute to those injustices. Advocacy seeks to promote human flourishing through systemic change. Reflecting on John Howard Yoder, Davis suggests that advocates should remember to focus on the persons who will be impacted by change so that advocacy remains a relational, Christian endeavor.[4]

The concept of "orchestration of prosocial motives" is an attempt to influence those in power to act morally. Daniel Batson observes:

> The potential for the greatest good may come from lead-
> ership strategies that orchestrate prosocial motives so that
> the strengths of one can overcome weaknesses of another.
> Strategies that combine appeals to either altruism or collec-
> tivism with appeals to principles seem especially promising.[5]

While justice may be a powerful motivator, Batson suggests that it is limited by its vulnerability to being both ignored and rationalized. Batson argues that altruism and collectivism may be effective, but are limited, because they focus on specific persons or groups. However, he suggests that the combination of these prosocial motives can overcome the weaknesses of each, thereby leading to positive social change.

Jones engaged world leaders often, addressing many different situations. Jones's aim was to advocate on behalf of those who had little public voice, and, consequently, to orchestrate prosocial motives in world leaders. As early as 1912 Jones began to focus his work of evangelism among the educated and Indian elites; in 1918 he acknowledged this direction in writing.[6] Over the course of his ministry, Jones continued to work among those in leadership in India and also developed relationships with ambassadors, diplomats, presidents, governors, senators, and other government officials.

His goal was not simply to provide another voice in these already crowded places of influence. Rather he worked diligently to provide a Christian witness. Jones believed he, along with other Christians, had a responsibility to influence those in power through public and private correspondence as well as personal conversation. His practices provide insight into how Christians today might engage those in leadership in the present time.

Foundation for Advocacy and Orchestrating for Change

It is important to distinguish the kind of advocacy and orchestration that might be associated with secular movements. While these movements may share many of the same goals as many Christian movements (such as a concern for the poor, giving voice to the voice-less, and uplifting the marginalized), they often do so from different starting points. As Christians, our public witness should emanate from the character formed through a life-transforming relationship with Christ. John Wesley struggled with the connection between Christian witness and Christian character in his sermon *The General Spread of the Gospel*. Wesley concludes that witness is integrally linked to char-acter. The "grand stumbling block" to the gospel, he argues, is "the lives of Christians."[7] Unless a Christian's life is transformed from the inside out, her public witness, and therefore her ability to orchestrate and advocate, may be not only fruitless but actually harmful to the spread of the gospel.

Jones incorporated Wesley's thought into his life and ministry. Jones's Christian character, empowered by the Holy Spirit, freed him to become a catalyst for change rather than a stumbling block to the gospel. The foundation for his advocacy and orchestration was estab-lished during his youth, at the altar of Memorial Methodist Church, and nurtured by Miss Nellie Logan, Jones's first-grade teacher. It was this same foundation that deepened at Asbury College and drove him to India to begin his missionary work in 1907.

His ability to advocate and orchestrate was enhanced in particu-lar ways by the humility with which he approached those in power. While he never shied away from speaking the truth, he practiced active listening. As Graham observes regarding Jones's approach to evangelizing educated Indians, "Christians [need] to acknowledge and identify with the way Indians think."[8] A quintessential example of such a willingness to listen is Jones's own description of one of his first encounters with Gandhi:

> I went straight to the point: You are perhaps the leading Hindu of India. Could you tell me what you think we as Christians should do to make Christianity more naturalized in India, not a foreign thing, identified with a foreign gov-ernment, but a part of the national life-something which

contributes its power to India's uplift and redemption?"
He immediately replied: "I would suggest four things: First
that all you Christians, missionaries and all, must begin to
live more like Jesus Christ. Second, that you practice your
religion without adulterating it, or toning it down. Third,
that you emphasize love and make it your working force,
for love is central in Christianity. Fourth, that you study the
non-Christian religions more sympathetically to find the
good in them, to have a more sympathetic approach to
the people.[9]

Jones shows a willingness here to engage the perspective of other
cultures and their leaders' wisdom. Not only did Jones listen to
Gandhi's advice, but he acted upon it by striving to live like Christ and
by taking a "sympathetic approach" to people of other cultures. This
posture of humility was not simply a means to an evangelistic end.
Jones earnestly desired to understand those whom he hoped would
come to Christ.

This attitude of humility extended not only to those he was serving but most especially to God. Jones's ultimate goal was to spread
the gospel, and he believed that God's mission through prevenient
grace was already, simultaneously, at work in the world. In Jones's
book, *The Christ of the Indian Road*, he notes:

Many who have looked for the Kingdom to come only by
observation so that they could say "Lo, here," and "Lo,
there," have been disappointed to find it come so slowly,
but the more discerning have suddenly awakened to find
that the Kingdom was in the midst of them and all around
them. Christianity is actually breaking out beyond the borders of the Christian Church and is being seen in most un-
expected places. If those who have not the spirit of Jesus
are none of his, no matter what outward symbols they
possess, then conversely those who have the spirit of Jesus
are his, no matter what outward symbols they may lack.
In a spiritual movement like that of Jesus it is difficult and
impossible to mark its frontiers. Statistics and classifications

lose their meaning and are impotent to tell who are in and who are not. Jesus told us it would be so.[10]

Jones seems clear that God's mission moves forward, perhaps in spite of Christians and the Christian church. He further observes, "[Christ] not only accomplishes for us in the past, he accompanies with us in the present. He is no spent force." This attitude of humility, and sense of his own limitations, made it clear to Jones that it is God who converts and finds those who are lost, not the evangelist alone. In his writing, Jones proclaims that he saw Christ at work in the world in surprising places. Reflecting on his work in India, he asserts, "I find him in places and movements I had never dreamed of and by the quiet sense of his presence he is forcing modification everywhere."[11] While the work of the evangelist is important, it is ultimately the work of God.

Given his self-awareness and clear, level assessment of others, we shouldn't be surprised that Jones was also a realist. Jones did not claim to be a realist in the sense of optimism on the one hand or pessimism on the other. Rather, his conviction of realism was related to his conviction and observation that God is at work in the world. In both his autobiography and an address at Asbury Theological Seminary in 1968, Jones recalls a conversation with a Russian actress, which prompted him to investigate whether he was an idealist or a realist. The actress said, "You are religious because you are weak. You turn to God for comfort. Do you want someone to hold your hand?" Jones responded:

> I am afraid you are Wrong [sic]. I don't turn to God for comfort, but for adequacy. I don't want God to hold my hand; I want him to strengthen my arm so I can lift a helping hand to others. I don't want him to wipe my tears; I want him to give me a handkerchief that I might wipe the tears of others. I repeat—I turn to God not for comfort, but for adequacy to meet whatever comes.[12]

Then, in a parting comment, the Russian actress accuses Jones of being an idealist. In Jones's address from 1968 he explains, "I went to my Bible to see if I was an idealist or a realist." Jones was drawn to the incarnation in Scripture. It was through the incarnation that Jones began to see, "[Jesus] was the revealer of reality." Furthermore, "I saw the Christian faith was realism."[13] This sense of Christianity's realism made Jones see the need to engage the world around him. While Jones did not use the term prevenient grace, he seemed to believe that God was already at work in the world, and thus our responsibility is to become coworkers with God in God's mission.

In addition to an attitude of humility, Jones's identity in Christ enabled him to interact with others in a way that was respectful and loving. His famous three-finger symbol, which proclaimed "Jesus is Lord," exemplifies this grounding identity as a subject of the King of kings. In his autobiography Jones describes how he decided that he "would know nothing but Jesus Christ and him crucified before that great non-Christian world."[14] Finding his identity in faith empowered Jones to address societal leaders with quiet confidence, knowing that it was not ultimately his authority that mattered but the authority of the Lord of all creation. Since Jones understood Christ to be the Lord, his ministry emphasized the importance of the Kingdom.

Stephen Graham suggests that by 1941 Jones began to see the universal and geopolitical application of the Kingdom of God, even in terms of US foreign policy. Graham notes that in Jones's article in *Christian Century*, "America's Role in This Crisis," Jones reveals his conviction that America should exercise its power as a mediator over and against the roles of participant or arbitrator. In this article Jones argues that participating in war would lead to a Russian-dominated peace due to the exhaustion of America and the relative non-exhaustion of Russia. Jones asserts, "The common people, seeing Russia as the only non-belligerent, will turn to her as the messiah to lead them out of this recurring hell of war and depression."[15] Jones argues that if the United States were to take on the role of arbitrator, it would be forced to make black-and-white decisions in a war where there is "no completely black and completely white." Rather than laying the foundations for peace, such a role could lay "the foundations of another clash."[16] In Jones's mind, this leaves one choice—that of mediator. Based on Ephesians 2:15, Jones goes on to argue that America's role should be to get each side, "to change and thus come to a third position, beyond each and yet gathering up the truth in each. In doing so, he usually lays the foundations of a lasting peace."[17] Jones was convinced that the Kingdom of God is a reality (realism).

Whether or not Jones was successful in his engagements with those in power, if Christian leaders seek to engage the individual and collective struggles of our day, it is essential that they work from the same faithful foundation as Jones. As Gandhi advised Jones, if we wish to be more effective in spreading Christianity and advocate and orchestrate for change, we should first strive to be more like Jesus.

Practices of Advocacy and Orchestration for Change

Jones uses his writing, his speaking, and his conversations with persons in power to bring about positive change. Using both advocacy and orchestration as a lens, he appeals to a combination of justice and altruism as he lobbies those in power. Before the outbreak of World War II, Jones develops relationships with many Japanese people. In an attempt to advocate for the Chinese people and orchestrate the motives of Japan, he circulates a letter following the 1931 Japanese invasion of Manchuria. In response to this act of aggression, Jones writes "An Open Letter to Japan," in which he demonstrates his desire to exercise moral leadership on the world stage:

> We are all in deep need, the writer along with the rest. But—and this is the point—the central international crime that is being committed in the world today is the crime of the invasion of China by your people. It is a crime against China, against international peace, against your own best interests, and against what you might have been to the rest of us. Go back and be the kind of Japan you might

have been had you not missed the turning of the road, and we will follow you and receive from you. Now we can receive nothing. As long as this Wrong to China continues we can receive from you neither culturally, nor morally, nor spiritually, and it may be that we shall be compelled to say, economically. And we say this with a heavy heart, for we are saying it to friends.[18]

In this letter Jones appeals to peace, justice, and the interest of Japan. However, he also appeals to the compassion of the Japanese through his belief that, at its best, Japan has much to offer the world; he forcefully argues that the invasion has damaged that potential.

Writing to President Roosevelt during the height of World War II, Jones presses Roosevelt concerning Indian independence and boldly challenges the sitting president to press Britain to extend self-rule to India as they had with Canada, Australia, and South Africa. Jones writes, "The real test of whether freedom is to be given to a person as a person, or to a person as a white person only, has now come."[19] Jones addresses the president personally and forcefully:

The only man who can head that off is you, Mr. President. Some of us are deeply disappointed that you have not done it before this. You are usually foresighted and bold. But here you have failed. . . . This, then, is the key: Say the forward-looking word of liberty for everybody and you go up; say the hesitating, backward-looking word and you go down. The American public is ready, apparently, to respond to something that will lay the foundations of the new world order for everybody.[20]

We can see here that Jones's main concern in advocacy is God's justice and to secure liberty for all persons.

His writings on behalf of the Japanese political prisoners in Sugamo Prison following World War II are particularly exemplary of his moral leadership. Writing to John Foster Dulles, US Secretary of State, in 1953, Jones declares:

I do not know the relative guilt or innocence of these men. I only know that they were caught in the passions of war and were tried when it was difficult to get a fair and impartial trial. . . . May I suggest one of two things: First, that Christian forgiveness be exercised and the prisoners freed and Sugamo wiped out. Let it be buried with the past. Second, if that cannot be done, then why not turn the whole matter over to the Japanese Government and trust them to deal with the whole matter in a way they think best. The trusting of the Japanese Government with the responsibility of settling the question would show our faith in their sense of responsibility and fair-mindedness.

I hope that one of these alternatives may be chosen and chosen quickly. If not, then Sugamo is a festering sore, breeding bitterness and discontent and accomplishing nothing that I can see.

When you were here before about the Peace Treaty, Admiral Nemura said to me, "Mr. Dulles does not seem like a diplomat trying to come to diplomatic conclusions. He seems more like a Christian seeking a Christian solution to this very important matter. It is a left-over and should be wiped out as soon as possible. Forgiveness would heal. Revenge will keep the wound open."[21]

Jones's orchestration and advocacy for the men remaining in Sugamo Prison appeals to both the Christian characteristic of forgiveness as well as the known Christian character of Secretary Dulles. Jones also couches his proposal in a future-oriented view in which healing might take place rather than preserving wounds that might result in further punishment and conflict. In addition, he appeals to the wisdom of trusting the Japanese government as a way to move forward from the damage of the war.

These are just a few of many examples. Jones advocated and orchestrated for change based on Christian discipleship, which entailed humility, a strong sense of identity in and through Christ, and a belief that the Kingdom of God was real and universally applicable.

Leading through Advocacy and Orchestration: Lessons for Today

Are Christians forced to choose between retreat and political engagement, or is there an alternative way of thinking about how we engage with the world while maintaining our identity in Christ? Jones's writing does not suggest that he saw a conflict between his commitment to evangelism and his commitment to engage world leaders on important issues. In fact, he seems to have understood both as part of a holistic approach to bringing the gospel to the world. Jones's approach works in a pluralistic society through humility, awareness of motives, openness to listening, strength of identity in Christ, and interactions, which combine advocacy with his orchestration of change. While methods of communication have changed, this approach is still potent in the context of relationship. Just as in Jones's day, systemic as well as personal spiritual issues need attention. We need Jones's combined structural and individual approach now more than ever. We live in a world that is more connected in some ways than Jones's world, yet more divided at both systemic and personal levels in others.

Jones's advocacy and orchestration was possible only because he was not afraid to offend people. However, if people were offended, he wanted them to be offended by the person of Christ, not the person of E. Stanley Jones. Jones believed that advocacy and orchestration was often not looked upon kindly by those in power. Stephen Graham reports that Jones was visited by the FBI in 1944, as a result of a letter he had written on behalf of a group of Christian ministers. The letter pressed the issue of hunger in Europe during the closing days of WW II. Documents declassified in 2011 indicate that Jones, including his postal correspondence, was observed by the government. In one report, the United States government was concerned about Jones's correspondence with Japanese persons as well as the use of the term "Ashram," which the examiners connected with Hinduism (not understanding that this was a Christian Ashram).[22] In another report, government officials focused on "reprehensible statements" regarding the war with Japan. They were concerned that Dr. Jones was partially blaming American policy for Japanese aggression.[23] Fortunately for Jones these investigations did not result in punitive actions. Jones's trials and tribulations should not serve as a deterrent to doing what is right; rather, they are a stark reminder of the potential cost of advocacy and orchestration for Christian leaders.

Rather than retreat from political activism, Jones's ministry proves that we can engage in advocacy and orchestration without compromising our character as children of the King of kings. As we engage in such work, we earn a hearing for the gospel, knowing that ultimately it is Jesus who will transform the hearts of men and women. Jones's final words in his autobiography sum it up well:

> After reviewing the world of human events for sixty years in East and West, North and South, and after trying this Way for sixty years, I am prepared to say that I see no way out of the world's misery and the world's emptiness, both in the individual and in the collective, except the way that "this Jesus," now present and now available, offers in his own person—a person who embodied the "Kingdom which cannot be shaken" and is himself the unchanging Person, "the same yesterday, today and forever," and who when you find him will bring you the Father—the Eternal God. "Jesus is Lord!"[24]

The life and ministry of E. Stanley Jones calls us to engage with the world around us, including those in leadership, out of a relationship with the "unchanging person" of Jesus and as a citizen of His "Unshakable Kingdom."[25]

From the examples above we learn from Jones the importance of correspondence, conversation, and open letters to impact the public square. Like Jones, we can use correspondence to write with love and compassion to individuals, advocating and orchestrating in a prosocial manner for change. As Christians we must do so in a way that does not denigrate the person to whom we are communicating but which calls the individual to higher moral behavior. We can also write open letters to the community, such as in a contemporary op-ed or blog post. Jones teaches us to relate to others in ways that do not attack or try to embarrass, while still calling people to account for their actions and to live in light of Jesus's reign. All these options remain open to us as we engage the public square. Like Jones, we must do so with humility and with the intention to promote the gospel for the sake of the Kingdom. It is not about our agenda but being willing to participate in God's agenda.

PUBLIC WITNESS

Kimberly D. Reisman

Though I never met him, the spirit of Eli Stanley Jones animated my home as I grew up.

In 1963 my father was leading a prayer group at Trinity Methodist Church in Gulfport, Mississippi. As part of their devotional time, they were reading Jones's book, *In Christ*. My father had been embroiled in the racial turmoil of those times, especially in the life of the Methodist Church in Mississippi. The book had a profound effect on him, and he decided to invite a friend to accompany him to one of Jones's Ashrams in Florida.

In the aftermath of that experience, my father invited Jones to lead an Ashram in Mississippi. He booked a Methodist conference facility and began publicizing the event; however, because Jones would speak only at events that were open to everyone, the conference center cancelled their commitment. He booked another conference facility—one owned by what was then the Central Jurisdiction—but the public opposition was too great. The event had to be cancelled completely.

During this time, my father was also gathering privately with three other young Mississippi clergymen, drafting a statement that would be known as *Born of Conviction*. It was signed by twenty-six clergymen, most of whom were under the age of thirty. In it, they publicly declared their support of the civil rights movement and an end to segregation—in the church, in education, and in society at large.

The uproar following the release of *Born of Conviction* made it impossible to remain in Mississippi; and, because Bishop Gerald Kennedy was one of the few Methodist bishops who would accept us, my family moved to California. However, before leaving, Jones invited my father to join him in Scandinavia for three weeks, teaching young adults at various Ashrams in that region. Then, in 1968, both my parents were able to be with him in India, where a photo of Jones and my parents was taken, each of them holding up three fingers in his classic sign: Jesus. Is. Lord. That photo and a framed flyer announcing the failed Mississippi Ashram have sat on my father's desk for as long as I can remember.

E. Stanley Jones shaped my family in powerful ways. In particular, his emphasis on public speaking shaped both my father's and my own understanding of preaching. We were not alone in this experience; Jones's reach went far beyond my family circle. Despite our time being a full century after his ministry began, Jones's practice of public lectures offers wisdom to those who seek an effective evangelistic witness in the midst of a religiously plural landscape. Examining that wisdom, as well as its implications for ministry today, is the focus of this chapter.

Public Lectures

As noted in a number of essays in this volume, public lectures (often a series of lectures over a number of days), followed by a period of question-and-answer time, played a vital role in Jones's ministry and became a critical way in which Jones witnessed to the story of God in Christ in public. Sometimes the gatherings included community forums, panel discussions, and informal gatherings where diverse groups of people came together for dialogue. But the public lecture followed by a time of questions and answers became a hallmark of Jones's ministry in India.

A pattern to these public gatherings developed over time. Jones would establish relationships with various leading figures in a specific city or area, and they would issue invitations and publicly promote the lectures, which would take place not in churches but in open, public spaces, town halls, Hindu and Christian college auditoriums, even Hindu temple compounds. A number of important attributes undergirded these lectures and shed light on the ministry philosophy behind this aspect of Jones's work.

First, Jones believed that the process of nurturing those who were already Christian could go hand in hand with evangelizing non-Christians. The public lectures typically took place in the evening, but on lecture days Jones typically reserved the morning for meeting with Christians in the area. The purpose of these gatherings was to strengthen their commitment to Christ, increase their responsiveness to spiritual power, and enhance their awareness of the "joyous privilege of soul-winning."[1] The focus was on the Christian community. The public lectures in the evening, however, focused on the non-Christians who made up most of the audience. In these lectures Jones spoke about Jesus and faith in Him and invited people to reflect and respond. Jones believed that Christians cannot share their faith with grace and confidence, whether publicly or privately, if they are not thoroughly in touch with the life-giving tenets of Christian faith. In other words, to be an effective evangelist one must first be a practicing disciple.

Second, Jones's approach implies that people who are considering Christ need space to dialogue and converse about the gospel. In order to facilitate this dialogue, Jones offered a question-and-answer period at the end of each evening lecture. Sometimes the questions were written ahead of time, but often they came directly from the audience. He was committed to facing these questions regardless of the difficulty. He took each seriously and did not try to evade or dismiss them as trivial.

Finally, Jones believed that evangelism resembles less the characteristics of a lawyer and more that of a witness. For Jones, the purpose of the lectures was not to defend God or justify God but to witness to the story of God in Christ. Jones believed that God does not desire us to argue God's case before the court of the world; God desires that we be witnesses who tell the truth about what we have seen, heard, and experienced. Therefore, on the last night of a lecture series, Jones shared his personal experience of Christ. He wanted people to hear his personal story of faith, how he came to faith, and why he believed in Jesus and gave his life to Him.

Parallels between Early Twentieth-Century India and Twenty-First-Century U.S.

Our world is a different place than it was in Jones's day; yet clichéd as it may be, the saying remains true: the more things change, the more they stay the same. Humans continue to experience spiritual hunger. We continue to search for something beyond ourselves to fill the God-shaped hole within each of us, and options continue to abound for filling that gap. Furthermore, the spiritual landscape in the United States today resembles the India of Jones's day in several specific and remarkable ways.

Though Christianity is not presently, nor ever has been, a minority voice in the United States in the way Jones experienced it in India, Christianity is facing a significant crisis of both identity and integrity in the eyes of those beyond the church. This, along with the generally polarized quality of current American public discourse, has led to a substantial weakening of our voice. Recent research indicates that though 78 percent of Americans identify themselves as Christian, 44 percent of Americans qualify as "post-Christian," based on a set of criteria ranging from identifying as atheist to whether they have read the Bible in the last week.[2] Further, there is an emerging category of "spiritual but not religious" adults, many of whom believe, in contrast to practicing Christians, that religion is *mostly harmful*.[3] This data, coupled with the long-discussed view of many unchurched Americans that Christians are hypocritical, judgmental, sheltered, and too political,[4] has created an environment where Christians cannot assume a receptive audience for their public witness. We find ourselves, interestingly, in a similar position to the one in which Jones found himself in India. We lay claim to a powerful gospel, yet fewer and fewer people feel any cultural need to attend to it. This is a reality few Christians are used to experiencing, which has led, in many instances, to either an unattractively defensive posture or an aggressively offensive one, neither of which engenders a positive hearing for our message. In this kind of environment, attending to our way of being in the world—our posture—as we engage in public witness is of crucial importance, and Jones's example is both significant and timely.

In light of the similarities, it is not surprising that some of the challenges Jones faced as he evangelized India resemble some of those faced by evangelists in the United States today. Jones outlines several of these challenges in his landmark work, *The Christ of the Indian Road*. First and foremost, he identifies a problem that has plagued Western Christians for centuries, namely an air of religious superiority. Jones expresses his concern with this attitude when he writes, "Around the world the problem of Christian work is the problem of the Christian worker."[5] He recognizes that the attitude of the evangelist is often a detriment to the work of the evangelist. The assumption of superiority was the mistake of the missionaries who preceded Jones, believing they needed to attack the weaknesses of other religions and then establish Christianity on the ruins.[6] We can see vestiges of this attitude in the derisive stance some Christians take toward those beyond the church. Franklin Graham's harsh rhetoric, calling Islam a "very evil and wicked religion" that directs people to beat their wives and murder their children if they commit adultery is a vivid example. Though Graham declares he has Muslim friends and "love[s] the people of Islam," his rhetoric comes across very differently than Jones's approach.[7] So often in evangelism we believe that to build Christianity up, we must tear others down. Jones believed this was not only unnecessary but actually unhelpful to the task of evangelism.

Jones's Posture of Evangelism

Much of my work has focused on articulating a Christian posture for sharing faith. Christian evangelists are most effective in their ministry when they model an authentic "way of being," or what I refer to as "posture," that embodies the gospel story. I believe such a posture includes six essential values of authentic evangelism: humility, clarity, prayer, integrity, worship, and urgency.[8] This posture is evident in all truly effective evangelists, and Jones is no exception. He provided an exemplary example, especially in the context of public witnessing. Though all of these values are plainly evident in Jones's ministry, three are of particular interest to the subject of this chapter and book: humility, clarity, and integrity.

Jones was known, for example, for his *humility*. Even as he affirmed Christ as Lord in a religiously plural landscape, Jones was quite humble in tone. This tone enabled him to overcome both an attitude of superiority and a fear of causing offense, a phenomena David Bosch aptly describes as "bold humility."[9] For example, early in Jones's work, as he lay down the principles that would guide him, he determined that he would never malign other faiths. To that end, he announced at the beginning of his public lectures that there would be no attack upon another's religion. If there was to be any attack in his presentation, he resolved that

> it must be by the *positive* presentation of Christ. He himself must be the attack. That would mean that *that kind of an attack may turn in two directions—upon us as well as upon them. He would judge both of us.* This would tend to save us from feelings and attitudes of superiority, so ruinous to Christian work.[10]

The result was a ministry defined by a commitment to Christ without demeaning other religious traditions.

Another value that is clearly evident in Jones's evangelistic practices is his *clarity* in presenting the gospel story. He refused to camouflage the meaning or purpose of his public lectures. Jones believed his audience should always know what they were coming to hear. The effectiveness of this honest and clear approach was confirmed on many occasions as he witnessed frustration on the part of listeners when other Christian speakers would avoid talking directly about their faith. For Jones, the people of India already had many thoughts about God. It was about Christ that they knew little. The same might be said of the pluralistic US culture of our day. There are many thoughts about God, but it is Christ that needs to be proclaimed.

Because both humility and clarity defined Jones's posture, he was frequently seen as broad-minded in his own thinking when it came to God's truth in the world, while at the same time being "narrow" in his commitment to Christ. On the one hand, he sought truth wherever it could be found. He was "grateful for any truth found anywhere, knowing that it [was] a finger post that [pointed] to Jesus, who is the Truth."[11] This generous view of non-Christian religious philosophies and traditions was grounded in his commitment to the absoluteness of Jesus. When a Hindu commented that he was a "broad-minded Christian," Jones replied, "My brother, I am the narrowest man you have come across. I am broad on almost anything else, but on the one supreme necessity for human nature I am absolutely narrowed by the facts to one—Jesus."[12] Because he stood firmly on the conviction that Jesus is the center of the moral and spiritual universe, he was able to recognize, and thank God for, the laudable things in other cultures, religions, and thought. Jones's posture of evangelism helped him reach thousands of Indians and perhaps millions of people around the world through his public lectures. Contemporary evangelists would be wise to consider his posture and incorporate it into their own life of discipleship.

Lessons for Today

I believe we can discern a number of insights and lessons from Jones's public lectures that are especially relevant to ministry in religiously plural communities today. Many of these are interrelated, and together they point to the posture that is imperative for authentic evangelism in both personal and public contexts.

The first lesson is Jones's focus on presenting Christ rather than "Christianity" or even the church. Jones recognized that "the gospel lies in the person of Jesus, that he himself is the Good News."[13] Therefore, Christ was the focal point of all public lectures. Christianity was defined by Christ Himself, not by Western civilization or the cultural systems that may have been built around Him. Jones even avoided using the term *Christianity* as he publicized his public lectures, because the word was not found in Scripture, and in his mind, it created more confusion than clarity. This is a significant distinction that would serve us well in our current cultural context.

Second, Jones believed that personal and corporate embodiment of the gospel undergirds the announcement of the gospel that took place in public lecture. In other words, as the church announced Christ, it had to also model Christ. As he watched faith in Jesus Christ breaking out beyond the borders of the Christian church, he wondered:

> Will the present Christian Church be big enough, responsive enough, Christlike enough to be the medium and organ through which Christ will come to India? . . . Will the Christian Church be Christlike enough to be the moral and spiritual center of this overflowing Christianity?[14]

He recognized that "ancient rituals and orders, and power at court and correctly stated doctrine avail little if Christlikeness is not the outstanding characteristic of the life of the people of the churches."[15] At the heart of his concern was a truth that cuts across time and place: when people catch a glimpse of the Spirit of Jesus, and begin to gain an understanding of what it means to be a follower of Christ, they begin to judge the church, and Christians, in that light. As individual Christians, and as the church, we are always judged by "the religion we avow and by the Christ whom we profess to follow."[16]

Jones believed that both an individual's witness and the church's public witness are intimately connected to personal and corporate embodiment of the gospel. He recognized the importance of *integrity* (the third essential value listed above) to effective and authentic evangelism. Our words must ring true to our lives, and our lives must reinforce our words. We will not be able to effectively witness in the public arena if our public witness—our way of being in the world—does not align with the content of our public witnessing. A profound conversation with Mahatma Gandhi drove this point home to Jones. After sharing his desire that Christianity no longer be identified as foreign but become a natural part of the spiritual landscape of India, Jones asked Gandhi what he must do to make that possible. Gandhi's reply was shared in the last chapter and is worth repeating here:

> I would suggest, first, that all of you Christians, missionaries and all, must begin to *live more like Jesus Christ*. . . . Second, I would suggest that you must *practice your religion without adulterating or toning it down*. . . . Third, I would suggest that you must put your emphasis upon love, for *love is the center and soul of Christianity*. . . . Fourth, I would suggest that you study the non-Christian religions and culture more sympathetically in order to find the good that is in them, so that you might have a more sympathetic approach to the people.[17]

This advice is as valid now as it was then. At their most foundational level our lives must fully reflect the one we follow. More specifically, in the spiritually diverse culture of the United States, we reflect Jesus—the one who took the time to know people and their needs—by being willing to learn about, engage, and respect those who may live and believe differently than we do. Additionally, as we share our faith, teach it to our children, and learn to be disciples with fellow Christians, there is great danger, as Jones well realized, in "inoculating the world with a mild form of Christianity" and thus making it "immune against the real thing." He believed the antidote was to present the gospel in all its "rugged simplicity and high demand"; to recognize love as "the working force, the one real power in a moral universe"; and that it should be "applied between individuals and groups and races and nations, the one cement and salvation of the world."[18]

The fruitfulness of any isolated instance of public witness on behalf of Jesus Christ is irrevocably intertwined with the overall integrity of our corporate public witness as the Body of Christ. We may have the opportunity to make a public witness for Christ in a community setting or other environment, but that will always be undergirded, for better or for worse, by the overall public witness of the community of faith—our overarching posture, our communal way of being in the world.

One of the chapters in *The Christ of the Indian Road* is significantly named "The Great Hindrance." In that chapter Jones identifies racism as one of the greatest threats to the proclamation of the gospel:

> The Hindus have discovered that Jesus looked on man apart from race and birth and color. . . . They know that he was color blind and that the vision that he saw and that he aimed to transmit to others was that there is "one race, one color and one soul in humanity." In the white light of that conception they are judging us.[19]

In 1925 Jones saw the need for national and racial repentance on the part of Christians in the West. This was one of the ministry-shaping things about Jones that impacted my parents in the 1960s. Today, the Indian critique continues to reverberate: "We must be Christian, but Christian in a bigger, broader way than we have hitherto been."[20]

The evil of racism remains one poignant example of the church's ongoing struggle to embody the gospel. If the church fails to embody the gospel in this area and in others, such as the complexities of pluralism, polarizing partisanship, the blurring of the boundaries between Christianity and patriotism, and the sinful complicity of institutional Christianity and the political process, the world may just reject our primary witness to the lordship of Christ.

We should not be surprised by the link between embodiment and witness. Jones certainly was not. He recognized that the seeds of domination, war, and racism were present in the way the gospel was propagated throughout history.[21] And if we are honest about our history, we must admit this is not simply about how the gospel has been propagated. These seeds have had an even more profound effect, having taken root from the moment Christianity became entwined with notions of empire in the fourth century. They have grown insidiously in the centuries since, creating a need to develop the just-war theory, introducing the concept of the "infidel" and theologies of "the other," and even producing political concepts such as the doctrine of discovery,[22] which was one of the founding concepts of the United States Constitution and has continued to affect rulings by the Supreme Court.

Though it is not possible to fully explore this final implication of Jones's approach to public witnessing in this chapter, it is not controversial to say that Christianity's overall witness—as it has unfolded throughout history and as it continues to unfold in our present day—clearly influences, at the most profound level, the effectiveness of our public witness for Christ. The positive contributions of the church to human flourishing, for instance in the arena of health care and education, make our effort to witness for Christ in the public arena much easier. Yet the church's complicity in anti-gospel environments such as slavery, colonialism, environmental degradation, and postmodern imperialism, along with the continued presence of racism and sexism both within and outside of the community of faith, dramatically hinder our ability to find a receptive hearing in the public square. In light of this, we would do well to attend to Jones's observation about India, which applies with equal force to US culture in our own day:

> India is asking questions; those that she asks with her lips
> are serious and searching, but of far more vital concern are
> the silent weighing and inward judgments of us by which
> India comes to her conclusions about Christ.
>   The High Priest asked Jesus "of his disciples and of his
> teaching." The non-Christian world is asking those same
> two things and always in that order. "What life have you?"
> "What light have you?"[23]

As we seek to witness publicly on behalf of Jesus Christ, how will we answer?

A third lesson from Jones's public lectures that seems pertinent today is Jones's belief that witnessing to Jesus from within a religiously plural gathering may be more effective than witnessing to Him in isolation from other religious communities. Community forums featuring people from different faiths provide opportunities for mutual growth in understanding and respect as well as occasions to share about Jesus Christ. Collaborating with others on projects that benefit and promote the common good can provide safe spaces for mutual learning and sharing around issues of faith and religious practice. As relationships grow among people of different religions, invitations can be extended to engage in public conversations around issues of faith. The common thread in these and other similar scenarios is the emphasis on shared public space and relationship. Rather than taking place in a church environment (which in our day is considered private space), as might be the case in a preaching event, revival, or other traditionally understood evangelistic gathering, these examples underscore the importance of public space, where all might feel the comfort of common ground. Additionally, these examples assume a basic level of trust and respect as the foundation for relationship. When that trust and respect are evident and steadfast, space is created to share an undiluted gospel that embodies a posture rooted in the essential values of humility, clarity, and integrity, in keeping with the spirit of Jones's ministry.

A fourth lesson is deeply connected to some of the previous ones, namely that discipleship is both personal and corporate. Jones understood the necessity of a deep and lively sense of Christ's ongoing presence in our personal lives and in the life of the community of faith. This grounded both his commitment to nurturing and teaching the Christians in the cities he visited, and his concern about whether the church would be responsive and Christlike enough to engage the budding spirituality of India.

As in Jones's day, we must be in touch with our personal experience of Christ—the gift we have been given, undeserved and unmerited. Our inward experience of faith is the ground for our sharing in both personal situations and the public arena—not telling others what *they* should believe; but rather, telling them what *we* believe and what Christ has done in our own lives.[24] Further, the connection to our personal experience of Christ must include more than a future focus (eternal life), as important and life-giving as that may be. It must also include a lively awareness of the ways in which Christ is working in our daily lives. Our witness takes on greater depth and authenticity when our hope for a future life in God's new creation is intimately tied to our experience of life in God's present creation.

Additionally, because Christian salvation is both whole creation salvation and the salvation of the whole, individual experience is not complete without the communal dimension. An understanding of the communal dimension of Christian salvation emphasizes that God's Kingdom is not made up of individual souls, each independently reconciled to God yet isolated from one another. Christian salvation is the reconciliation of *all* things—all people, all creation, the entire universe. It is a communal reality in which our relationship with God is bound up with our relationship with others as well as with creation and our care of it. Without a clear understanding of *both* dimensions of salvation, any public witness will ring hollow, unsupported by our behavior and lacking the fullness of the gospel. In our current culture, when thinking about public witness, it may well be that a strong presentation of the communal nature of salvation would bear much fruit. Though intrigued by "meaning of life" oriented questions, non-Christians are less concerned or interested in the idea of life after death or what will happen to them personally when they die than they are with issues of faith in the context of community.[25]

Finally, Christians today can learn from Jones's conviction that Jesus was Himself the best witness to the gospel. Jesus did not need to be protected from critique or attack; He was His own witness. Rather than being protected, Jesus simply needed to be presented.[26] He, through His Spirit, speaks for Himself better than we ever can. Jones was willing to open himself to being questioned after every lecture because he believed in a profound truth: if people would go deep enough

> they would stand face to face with Jesus. For he did not come to bring a way of life—he came to be Life itself. . . . He did not come to bring a set of truths to set alongside of other truths, as some have superficially imagined, he came to be Truth; and if [people go] far enough with truth, it will lead [them] by the hand till [they face] him who is Truth itself.[27]

This is connected to the essential values of humility and clarity discussed earlier. We have the clarity to join Jones in claiming the truth that Jesus is the fulcrum on which all of creation rests, while at the same time humbly rejoicing whenever good is found in other human understandings of the life of the spirit.

This final lesson is a challenge in our day for two reasons, both of which relate to trust. The first is that many Christians do not trust they have the answers to questions they may be asked. Therefore, many are reluctant to share their faith, both privately and publicly. Like Jones, many of us feel that we must be God's lawyer, arguing every point, or mastering the various theological concepts that weave through Christian faith. Our perceived lack of mastery silences us from offering our own experiences of faith and allowing the Holy Spirit of Jesus to freely move. We may fear offending, looking foolish, or even saying something wrong. Non-Christians, however, are more receptive than we may believe and are often quite open to authentic sharing.[28] Our need, therefore, is to recognize that, rather than having all the answers, the greater necessity is a posture of humility and a willingness to walk with others toward a mutual discovery of the answers opened to us by the power of Christ's Holy Spirit.

The second reason this lesson is so challenging for many Christians today is that some simply do not trust that Jesus is able to be His own witness. A turning point for Jones was his realization that Jesus did not need to be protected, but could provide His own witness, if Jones would only present Him. In our day we seem to believe that Jesus needs the protection of our cultural constructs and our political systems. Some argue, for instance, if we would return (Christian) prayer to the public schools, Christianity would be reinforced (and our nation strengthened). It is as though Christians in the U.S. believe the power of the gospel comes more from the trappings of *Christendom* than from God the Father, who sent the Son, in the power of the Holy Spirit. Jones recognized nearly a century ago that Jesus is able to be His own witness. Jesus needs only our willingness—with clarity, humility, and integrity—to present Him and the gospel He inhabits.

Conclusion

The continued impact of E. Stanley Jones extends beyond the details of his method. We can be encouraged by his bold use of public lectures, his courageous openness to questioning, and his humble willingness to nurture the Christian communities he encountered. However, the timeless power of his legacy lies in the continuity of the posture he embodied in every context in which he worked, a posture grounded in humility, clarity, and integrity. As we witness for Jesus Christ, in both the public arena and our personal relationships, Jones's example challenges us to pursue a deeper experience of Christ in our own lives, to open ourselves to aspects of goodness that reside in the wide variety of human understandings of the spiritual life, to recognize and combat the confusion of Christian faith and cultural constructs, and to proclaim without apology or dilution, that Jesus Christ is indeed the fulcrum point of all creation.

CONCLUSION

F. Douglas Powe Jr.

ndividuals are constantly talking about reclaiming our Wesleyan heritage. If we can simply be more like those involved in the early Wesleyan movement, then all of our problems will be solved. There are several issues with this ideal, but for our purposes let me focus on one. The thought that we can simply copy or emulate what John, Charles, or other early Methodists did in our current culture is naive. For instance, seeking to reach the masses by going out to preach in the fields like John Wesley disregards important issues, such as context. We are trying to copy a practice that worked under one set of circumstances and make it work for a different set of circumstances. Reclaiming our Wesleyan heritage in this manner is not helpful, because we are trying to commute practices from one context to another.

As pointed out in the introduction, there is another way of reclaiming our Wesleyan heritage, and this is what makes Jones so compelling today. Jones did not simply copy what John Wesley did; he contextualized field preaching for another context. I cannot highlight enough the importance of learning to contextualize like Jones. Too often I hear pastors and laypeople looking for the thing to do to solve the congregation's evangelistic issues. They go to a training event and hear someone say, "Our congregation started growing when we gave out refrigerator magnets with the church name on it," or some other similar, seemingly easy idea. These ideas become their new evangelistic outreach solution. Typically they do not work!

Jones understood the practice of field preaching, but he never focused on the activity as an end in and of itself. One of the goals of field preaching was building relationships with those whom the Church of England was not reaching. The idea of reaching out to intellectuals in India maintained the practice of field preaching in a way that contextualized it for the culture Jones was serving. Jones realized that the construct of the culture required starting with those whom most missionaries ignored. He did so by reclaiming the Wesleyan ideals of being relational, engaging, and dialogical, altering the practice of field preaching in the process to fit his context.

It is my hope that readers of this text have learned many things, but, if nothing else, the importance of contextualizing practices. It is a mistake to simply copy or emulate what someone else has done or is doing. What is necessary is to understand the difference between the idea and the activity resulting from the idea. In the preceding chapters we have attempted to share both with you, as they relate to Jones and lessons we can learn for today. My focus in this conclusion is highlighting some of the ideals that have been shared in the chapters as a means of helping individuals to connect the dots to their contexts.

Ideals

Three ideals, which are explicit and implicit in the chapters, are that Jones was engaging, dialogical, and relational. If you reread each chapter through these lenses, typically two or all three of these ideals are expressed. Jones was comfortable engaging those who thought and believed differently than he did. In fact, Jones's public lectures included a question-and-answer time to engage those who thought and believed differently. The idea of engaging others who are different is something often talked about in various spaces, but we are not often successful at living it out.

In part, I believe this is because our focus on engaging tends toward two polar opposites. First, we seek commonality at all expense and gloss over our differences.[1] The second is that we shut down all conversation by demeaning those who disagree with us through labels. For example, we claim the *other* is liberal or conservative, progressive or traditionalist, etc. The implication is that they are not even worthy of engaging because we already know their perspective. Jones offers us an alternative between these polar opposites that requires us to engage the other as a child of God. For Jones this means all individuals must be taken seriously, even when they are very different from us. We take them seriously, realizing that we should not gloss over those differences or give in to demeaning the other as categorically *persona non grata*. The ideal of engaging all as children of God means altering the way we approach many people and creates a vulnerability that some of us are probably not comfortable expressing. For instance, Jones encouraged others to ask challenging questions about Christianity, not so he could demonstrate his skills of making points for Christ, but so he could demonstrate the point of creating a space where all perspectives where honored.

While Jones was engaging, he also was dialogical. By this I mean he encouraged dialogue. It has been pointed out in many of the aforementioned chapters that Jones held firmly to his belief in Christ. In fact, Jones was an exclusivist in that he understood salvation was possible only through Christ. Yet individuals who were not Christian were interested in having conversations with him. They did not perceive Jones as closed-minded.

Certainly, it is a tricky distinction to claim someone is exclusive in their beliefs but not closed-minded. If Jones's mind was already made up about Christ before he went into a conversation, how could he truly be open-minded? I think, in part, the challenge is how we often use *open-* and *closed-minded* today. Open-minded people are perceived to be accepting of others' beliefs. They do not think their beliefs take precedence in any form or fashion. Closed-minded people believe their perspective to be the best one. By this standard Jones was closed-minded.

If we rethink our understanding of open-mindedness, not in terms of having to accept the beliefs of another, but instead to appreciate the beliefs of another, I think we get closer to Jones's perspective. Jones was open to listening to all perspectives, but he was never swayed to believe anything else could replace the salvation found through Christ. To be clear, this was not a perfunctory listening but one of deeply talking with others around their experiences of the divine. He, of course, learned from these conversations, which is one of the reasons for the Christian Ashram. Jones did not enter into dialogue with an attitude of shutting others down, but with genuine interest in what they had to say.

The truth is we often claim to be open-minded in the first sense I described above, but we treat others in a cursory manner by not really listening to them. We are seeking either to make our own points against them or to avoid conflict at all cost, and we are unwilling to really engage them. Jones genuinely listened to others and learned from them. This is what a dialogical process can be if we are more intentional about entering into it with a similar mind-set to Jones.

Finally, Jones was extremely relational. The truth is that even when some Christians are engaging and dialogical, they are not relational. When individuals who think and believe differently than we do are not swayed to our perspective, some of us will stop being in relationship with them. The end goal is persuading them at all cost. Jones continued to be in relationship with individuals, like Gandhi, who were never persuaded to Christ. This did not mean he was not hoping they would ultimately be persuaded, but the relationship was not stipulated on them being persuaded.

We are called to be relational in this same manner, with a willingness to walk with people who do not hold to our beliefs. Jones's ability to relate to people in this manner made his efforts to engage and be in dialogue with others authentic. I believe even those who were not ultimately persuaded to see Christ as their Savior were impressed by his willingness to stay connected to them. Being in relationship with another is not about conformity, but about authentically seeing the person as a child of God, and treating that person as such, no matter the circumstances.

The ideals of being engaging, dialogical and relational are foundational to how Jones was able to contextualize the gospel in a pluralistic culture. These same ideals should inform how we contextualize the gospel in our ever-increasingly pluralistic culture. Like Jones, we are called to be engaging, dialogical, and relational with all individuals. This includes those with whom we find common ground and those who are categorically opposed to our beliefs. I hope you will consider seriously how it is you are thinking through these ideals in your ministry. All of us live in pluralistic contexts, from the South to the West. The question is, "How do we contextualize these ideals?"

Lessons for Today

All of the authors offered us various insights for what we can learn from Jones regarding being Christian in a pluralistic context. I am not going to repeat every insight, but I want to lift up three challenges to help us with the contextualization question. First, I challenge us to be more *accessible* to others. It is easy to paint a picture of society as "going to hell in a handbasket." For that reason we seem to feel that the best thing to do is to stick with those we know who are safe. We close ourselves off from those who are not like us. We build relationships only with those who think, look, and act like us. I am not suggesting one take this to the extreme and get involved with folks doing illegal things. I am suggesting we need to broaden our circles so that others will see that we are accessible.

If I talk about wanting to connect with soccer families and how important it is to find ways to develop relationships with them, it is not helpful if I do this from inside my church. With the exception of those families who attend, no one else may ever know of my desire to connect. I am not really accessible to those outside of my congregation. To be accessible to them, I need to hang out in places where those who play soccer attend. This may mean coaching a team or getting involved as a referee. The point is that I have to be accessible to others so that they can know I hope to engage, dialogue, and relate to them.

Jones was accessible to those in positions of power, like Dulles and Roosevelt. He also was accessible to those not familiar to many of us, like Kim Reisman's father, a pastor in Mississippi (see her chapter). Jones understood that participating in God's work of transformation requires being open to all of God's people. Jones took this seriously throughout his life.

We live in a culture where we often limit accessibility to those who run in similar circles with us. In many cases this is not intentional, but we never move outside of our comfort zones. Like Jones, we are called to move out of our comfort zones and to open ourselves up to being more vulnerable by being more accessible. This means being intentional about building relationships outside of our normal networks. With everything going on in our lives, this feels like just one more task, but it is essential if we hope to connect with those not in our current circle. I challenge us to be more accessible to those outside of our current circles.

Second, I challenge us to take seriously the need for becoming *vulnerable* in our contexts. It is one thing to be accessible, but then we have to be willing to be open to others. Jones did this with the Round Table Conferences and other practices for engaging those who thought and believed differently from him. He put himself and his beliefs out there to be scrutinized by others.

When we seek to apply the ideals (engaging, dialogical, and relational) learned by Jones, it is necessary that we also become vulnerable. Too often we take the safe route and do things that do not require us to expose ourselves. For example, a feeding ministry at our congregation can be a great ministry (and for some it is a way of being vulnerable), but it allows us to do ministry where we get to set the terms. Folks have to come to us, and we control the resources, especially financial resources. Jones made himself vulnerable to others by going into their spaces and opening himself up to be questioned. Again, the goal is not to copy the activity of Jones but to think about what it means for us to be vulnerable in our contexts. How can we be more intentional about entering into spaces that we do not control, so that those who believe differently will feel comfortable engaging, dialoguing, and relating to us? This is a challenge we must continually keep in front of us.

Finally, I challenge us to recognize the importance of *reciprocity,* giving to others and taking in from others. The work we are called to do should never be one-sided. Too many Christians either abuse their voices in the public square by trying to shut down all the other voices or do not speak up in the name of Christ because they do not want to offend. Neither is a reciprocal approach that simultaneously makes room for others and witnesses to the work of Christ taking place in our midst.

It is this balance, or reciprocal approach, that made Jones unique and offers us insights into finding ways to hear and share in the public square. Learning to make space for others so that their voices can be heard is critically important. As Christians, we cannot be afraid of letting others speak and voice opinions that may differ from ours. We also cannot be afraid to witness to the ways in which we see Christ transforming lives and communities. Like Jones, we do not have to put others down to accomplish this goal; we simply need to share how we have experienced Christ.

While Jones was an exclusivist, he practiced reciprocity in a way that drew others to him. Our challenge is to take reciprocity seriously and to find ways in our contexts to live it out. The goal should be for all of us in the church to be known, not simply as Christians, but as Christians who cherish the personhood of others. This would mean we exemplify reciprocity in a way that impacts positively on the lives of others.

Some practices that can aid us in making a difference in our contexts are being accessible, vulnerable, and reciprocal. In a pluralistic culture, not sticking with those just like us, opening ourselves up to others, and learning to share with and receive from others is critical. Pluralism is not new, and the need to share the gospel in an authentic manner with integrity is not new. What is new for many is seeking a way to be Christian that is not hegemonic or timid. Jones offers us such a witness, and in this book we have shared insights that will help individuals to navigate between hegemony and timidity. We have shared how individuals can contextualize the gospel *with* people and not *for* people. It is our hope that readers will take these challenges seriously as they work to transform lives and communities in a similar fashion to Jones.

NOTES

Introduction

1 Stephen A. Graham, *Ordinary Man, Extraordinary Mission: The Life and Work of E. Stanley Jones* (Nashville: Abingdon Press, 2005), 335–36.

2 Ibid., 292.

3 Ibid., 302.

4 E. Stanley Jones, *Mahatma Gandhi: An Interpretation* (Lucknow: Lucknow Publishing House, 1963), 13.

5 Graham, *Ordinary Man, Extraordinary Mission*, 367.

6 Ibid., 397.

7 S. Wesley Ariarajah, *Your God, My God, Our God: Rethinking Christian Theology for Religious Plurality* (Geneva: World Council of Churches, 2012), 67–68.

8 E. Stanley Jones, *Along the Indian Road* (New York: Abingdon Press, 1939), 116.

9 E. Stanley Jones, *Christ at the Round Table* (London: Hodder & Stoughton, 1928), 13.

10 Ibid., 272.

11 Jones, *Along the Indian Road,* 99.

12 Graham, *Ordinary Man, Extraordinary Mission*, 181–82.

13 Jones's writings are also important to his evangelistic ministry, but they differ in at least one important respect from these three practices. They do not intentionally include an element of conversations with non-Christian communities.

14 E. Stanley Jones, *The Christ of the Indian Road* (New York: Abingdon, 1925), 83.

15 Ibid., 132

16 Ibid., 123.

17 Ibid., 21–22.

18 Jones, *Along the Indian Road*, 36.

19 Jones, *Christ at the Round Table*, 15.

20 Ibid., 17.

21 Ibid., 19.

22 Ibid., 24.

23 Ibid., 23.

24 Richard W. Taylor, *The Contribution of E. Stanley Jones* (Madras: The Christian Literature Society, 1973), 10–11. Taylor argues that the Round Table Conferences were the only true place of interreligious conversation in India at the time.

25 Jones, *Christ at the Round Table*, 46.

26 Ibid., 17.

27 Graham, *Ordinary Man, Extraordinary Mission*, 13.

28 E. Stanley Jones, *7 December 1929 Circular letter,* unpublished (1929), cited in Graham, 197.

29 Jones, *Along the Indian Road*, 44–45.

30 Ibid., 189.

31 Graham, *Ordinary Man, Extraordinary Mission*, 144.

32 Ibid., 148.

33 Graham, *Ordinary Man, Extraordinary Mission*, 178–79.

34 Ibid., 179.

35 Jones, *Christ at the Round Table*, 22.

36 Graham, *Ordinary Man, Extraordinary Mission*, 181–82.

37 Jones, *Christ at the Round Table*, 21. Jones was convinced that the scientific method, with its emphasis on experimentation, verification, and sharing of results, justified emphasizing people's experiences of faith. Throughout his life, he was convinced that an experience of Christ was more fruitful than an experience of any other faith tradition.

Chapter 1

1 David J. Bosch, *Transforming Mission: Paradigm Shifts in Theology of Mission* (Maryknoll, NY: Orbis Books, 2011), 341–49.

2 E. Stanley Jones, *The Christ of the Indian Road* (New York: Abingdon, 1925), 35–36.

3 Stephen A. Graham, *Ordinary Man, Extraordinary Mission: The Life and Work of E. Stanley Jones* (Nashville: Abingdon Press, 2005), 46.

4 Jones, *Christ of the Indian Road*, 63.

5 Ibid., 25.

6 Ibid.

7 Ibid., 26.

8 Ibid.

9 Ibid., 27.

10 Ibid.

11 Ibid.

12 Ibid., 22.

13 Ibid., 22–24.

14 Round Tables are discussed at length elsewhere in this volume. However, I briefly touch upon them here for their importance to Jones's work in the pluralistic environment.

15 E. Stanley Jones, *Christ at the Round Table* (New York: Abingdon Press, 1928), 26.

16 Ibid.

17 Ibid., 26–27.

18 Richard W. Taylor, "The Legacy of E. Stanley Jones," *International Bulletin of Missionary Research* 6, no. 3 (1982): 103.

19 Jones, *Christ at the Round Table*, 21.

20 Ibid., 22.

21 Ibid.

22 Ibid., 24.

23 Ibid., 54.

24 Ibid.

25 Ibid.

26 Ibid., 54–55.

27 Ibid., 114.

28 Ibid., 20–21.

29 Ibid., 121.

30 Ibid.

31 Bosch, *Transforming Mission*, 195–96.

32 Andrew Pratt, "'Out of One, Many—within One, Many': Religious Pluralism and Christian Ecumenism in the United States," *Perspectives in Religious Studies* 42, no. 2 (Summer 2015): 144–45.

33 Robert Wuthnow, "Responding to the New Religious Pluralism," *Cross Currents* 58, no. 1 (Spring 2008): 50.

34 "U.S. Public Becoming Less Religious," Pew Research Center, November 3, 2015, 5, http://www.pew forum.org/2015/11/03/u-s-public-becoming-less-religious/.

35 Aleksandra Sandstrom and Becka A. Alper, "If the U.S. Had 100 People: Charting Americans' Religious Beliefs and Practices," Pew Research Center, December 1, 2016, http://www.pewresearch.org/fact-tank/2016/12/01/if-the -u-s-had-100-people-charting-americans-religious-beliefs-and-practices/. Also, Becka A. Alper and Aleksandra Sandstrom, "If the U.S. Had 100 People: Charting Americans' Religious Affiliations," Pew Research Center, November 14, 2016, http://www.pewresearch.org/fact-tank/2016/11/14/if-the-u-s-had -100-people-charting-americans-religious-affiliations/. Also see "U.S. Public Becoming Less Religious."

36 David Masci and Michael Lipka, "Americans May Be Getting Less Religious, but Feelings of Spirituality Are on the Rise," Pew Research Center, January 21, 2016, http://www.pewresearch.org/fact-tank/2016/01/21/americans-spirituality/.

37 Jones, *Christ of the Indian Road*, 40.

38 Ibid., 36.

39 Ibid., 37.

40 Gerardo Marti and Gladys Ganiel, *The Deconstructed Church: Understanding Emerging Christianity* (New York: Oxford University, 2014), 184–87.

41 Jones, *Christ of the Indian Road*, 41.

42 Ibid., 24.

43 Terry Muck, "Mission Trajectories in the Twenty-First Century," in *The State of Missiology Today: Global Innovations in Christian Witness*, ed. Charles Van Engen (Downers Grove, IL: IVP Academic, 2016), 186–87.

44 Jones, *Christ of the Indian Road*, 35.

45 Ibid., 27.

Chapter 2

1 E. Stanley Jones, *The Reconstruction of the Church—On What Pattern?* (Nashville: Abingdon Press, 1970), 10.

2 As Jones writes, on the eve of World War II, critical of the church's past and apparently present failures to prevent war, "The hope of the world is for Christianity to return to its original spirit and attitude, to disentangle itself and give its messenger to a stricken and confused world. The Christian Church has played the Judas to Christ and has betrayed His Spirit and has proved false to the very meaning of the Cross. The only hope for itself and the world is to regain the spirit of the Kingdom" (E. Stanley Jones, *The Choice Before Us* [New York: Abingdon Press, 1937], 130).

3 Graham Cray, Ian Mobsby, and Aaron Kennedy, *Fresh Expressions of Church and the Kingdom of God* (Norwich, UK: Canterbury Press, 2012), xiv.

4 Ibid.

5 See *Mission-Shaped Church: Church Planting and Fresh Expressions in a Changing Context* (New York: Seabury Books, 2004).

6 Jones, *Reconstruction*, 9.

7 Ibid.

8 Ibid.

9 David Bundy writes "There was little time for evangelism and the stress combined with internal conflict frequently provoked his temper. During this period, he sought with his personal efforts to energize the Methodist Church in India and to turn each pastor into an equally ambitious American-style evangelist. He himself recalled two decades later, 'I was more of a boss than a brother. . . .' The demands on him, complicated by tetanus and depression, led to a mental breakdown, and a furlough" (David Bundy, "The Theology of the Kingdom of God in E. Stanley Jones," *Wesleyan Theological Journal* 23, no. 1–2 (Spring–Fall 1988): 62–63.

10 E. Stanley Jones, *A Song of Ascents: A Spiritual Autobiography* (Nashville: Abingdon Press, 1968), 211.

11 Ibid., 110.

12 Jones, *Reconstruction*, 180. In his description of Jones's ministry, Douglas Strong makes the same point regarding Jones's "distinction between Christ and Christianity: The former was the Savior of all humanity; the latter the expression of religion within a specific culture" (Douglas Strong, *They Walked in the Spirit: Personal Faith and Social Action in America* [Louisville: Westminster John Knox Press, 1997], 82). This division was expressed in some of Jones's earliest work. In his 1928 book, *Christ at the Round Table*, Jones wrote, "Can we find universality in Christianity? If we mean by it the system that has built up around Christ, then I am not sure that we can. It has gathered up into itself many local, temporary, and limiting things. . . . The things that have plagued Christendom in the past and are now plaguing it in the present are the things that we have added to the gospel and the things that we have taken from it. The plagues of controversy and division and weakness will be largely lifted when we get back to the center—Christ" (E. Stanley Jones, *Christ at the Round Table* [New York: Abingdon Press, 1928], 290–92).

13 Jones, *Reconstruction*, 32.

14 Ibid., 164.

15 The Kingdom of God "was a reconstruction that would remake the economic, the social and political, the physical, the moral and spiritual, and the collective. . . . The whole of life is the area of its operation" (E. Stanley Jones, *Conversion* [Nashville: Abingdon Press, 1959], 245).

16 Jones, *Reconstruction*, 12.

17 Ibid., 121.

18 Ibid., 81–82.

19 Ibid., 181–82.

20 Ibid.

21 Ibid., 58.

22 E. Stanley Jones, "Where Madras Missed Its Way," *The Indian Witness* 69 (9 Feb. 1939): 86–87; also published in *The Christian Century* 56 (1939): 351–52, quoted in Bundy, "The Theology of the Kingdom of God . . . ," 70.

23 Jones, *Song of Ascents*, 384.

24 Jones's thoughts on potential models for the unity of the church are detailed in chapter 15 of *Reconstruction*, "What About the Unity of the Churches?" and in chapter 17 of *Song of Ascents*, "Will the Church Sing a New Song?"

25 Jones writes, "Everyone needs a close-knit fellowship to which he is responsible and which is responsible for him. I found it in the class meetings. . . . This class meeting, where we told our successes and failures, our joys and our problems, became for me the germ of an idea which has blossomed into a world movement—the Christian Ashram movement" (*Song of Ascents*, 42).

26 Strong, *They Walked in the Spirit*, 84.

27 Jones, *Song of Ascents*, 218.

28 Ibid.

29 Ibid., 222.

30 Ibid.

31 Ibid.

32 Ibid., 217.

33 Ibid., 222.

34 In the dedication of his 1937 book *The Choice Before Us,* Jones writes, "Dedicated with deep affection to the Sat Tal Ashram [Jones's original Ashram community], a loyal group gathered from many nations . . . who in their corporate relationships demonstrate, at least in miniature, the meaning of the Kingdom of God" (E. Stanley Jones, *The Choice Before Us* [Nashville: Abingdon Press, 1937], 5).

35 Jones writes, "We are not trying to pull people out of their churches to absorb their time and attention and loyalty in a movement outside the churches. This would be to weaken the churches. We try to send them back into the churches better persons, better pastors, and better officials and members. . . . The Ashram thus becomes not a separatist movement, but a permeative movement" (*Song of Ascents*, 226).

36 Ibid., 232.

37 Ibid.

38 Ibid., 232–33.

39 Ibid., 233.

40 Ibid.

41 Ibid., 222.

42 Stephen A. Graham, *Ordinary Man, Extraordinary Mission: The Life and Work of E. Stanley Jones* (Nashville: Abingdon Press, 2005), 354.

43 See Pew Research Center, "America's Changing Religious Landscape," accessed August 5, 2017, http://www.pewforum.org/2015/05/12americas-changing -religious-landscape/.

44 Graham Cray, "Communities of the Kingdom," in Cray, Mobsby, and Kennedy, *Fresh Expressions of Church and the Kingdom of God*, 18.

45 Ibid.

46 Ibid.

47 Rowan Williams, "Fresh Expressions, the Cross, and the Kingdom," in Cray, Mobsby, and Kennedy, *Fresh Expressions of Church and the Kingdom of God*, 4. For another helpful framing of Jones's concern for Kingdom in conversation with contemporary church leadership, see Douglas Ruffle, *A Missionary Mindset: What Church Leaders Need to Know to Reach Their Community* (Nashville: Discipleship Resources, 2016), especially chap. 8, "The Kingdom: Living and Breathing the Good News."

48 Williams, "Fresh Expressions . . . ," 4.

49 Ibid., 5.

50 Ibid., 4–5, emphasis original.

51 To this end, Williams rightly draws attention to the role of sacraments within the formation of innovative ecclesial community. He does this, not simply to keep new ecclesial communities tethered to the tradition, but, more significantly, as a means to keep God at the center of the church's common life and work (a concern Jones would surely share). Williams writes, "It may be surprising for some, but the truth is that when we have our sacramental teaching and practice clear, we are likely to have our transformational social vision clear as well." This is the case, he argues, because "the sacraments show us, bring us in touch with, the God who acts before any initiative on our part; so they show us a God who is free from our preoccupations and agendas. Communion with this God of freedom sets us free to be critics and remakers of our world in his name." Put differently, it is in sacramental life that the church comes to see the "Unchangeable Person" of Christ and is empowered to practice a way of life in an "Unshakeable Kingdom." See Williams, "Fresh Expressions . . ," 9–10.

52 Jones, *Reconstruction*, 118.

Chapter 3

1 E. Stanley Jones, *Victory Through Surrender* (Nashville: Abingdon, 1966), 14.

2 E. Stanley Jones, *The Christ of the Indian Road* (Nashville: Abingdon, 1925), 32.

3 E. Stanley Jones, *A Song of Ascents: A Spiritual Biography* (Nashville: Abingdon, 1968), 385.

4 Ibid., 111

5 Reinhold Niebuhr, *An Interpretation of Christian Ethics* (San Francisco: Harper & Row, 1935), 108, 110.

6 Ibid.

7 Ibid., 111.

8 Jones, *Christ of the Indian Road*, 6, 167.

9 E. Stanley Jones, *Is the Kingdom of God Realism?* (Nashville: Abingdon, 1940), 74–75.

10 Jones, *Song of Ascents*, 175.

11 E. Stanley Jones, *Conversion* (Nashville: Abingdon, 1959), 44.

12 Jones, *Is the Kingdom of God Realism?*, 75.

13 Jones, *Song of Ascents*, 243.

14 Ibid., 32.

15 Ibid., 175.

16 Richard W. Taylor, *The Contribution of E. Stanley Jones* (Madras: The Christian Literature Society, 1973), 27.

17 Jones, *Song of Ascents*, 28–29.

18 Jones, *Conversion*, 198.

19 Ibid., 35.

20 Ibid., 40–41.

21 Ibid., 241.

22 Jones, *Victory Through Surrender*, 14.

23 Jones, *Is the Kingdom of God Realism?*, 184–86.

24 Jones, *Victory Through Surrender*, 27, 29. Jones cited the following verses to illustrate the self-surrender that the New Testament demands: Luke 9:23, Gal. 2:19, and Rom. 12:1.

25 Jones, *Conversion*, 181.

26 Ibid., 222.

27 Jones, *Victory Through Surrender*, 57.

28 E. Stanley Jones, *Christ and Human Suffering* (Nashville: Abingdon Press, 1933), 190.

29 Jones, *Victory Through Surrender*, 48–49.

30 Jones, *Christ of the Indian Road*, 35.

31 Ibid., 50.

32 E. Stanley Jones, "To Proselytize or to Convert—Which?," in *Indian Witness* (June 18, 1931): 387.

33 Jones, *Is the Kingdom of God Realism?*, 265, emphasis original.

34 Jones, *Conversion*, 210–13.

35 Jones, *Song of Ascents*, 296.

36 Ibid., 40.

37 Ibid., 41.

38 Jones, *Is the Kingdom of God Realism?*, 194, emphasis original.

39 Jones, *Victory Through Surrender*, 107.

40 Jones, *Song of Ascents*, 385–86.

41 M. M. Thomas and T. K. Thomas, in Taylor, *Contribution of Jones*, vii.

42 Jones, *Song of Ascents*, 256–57.

43 Jones, *Is the Kingdom of God Realism?*, 203, 272.

44 Jones, *Song of Ascents*, 42–43.

45 Ibid., 67.

46 Ibid., 96.

47 Ibid., 133–34.

48 Jones, *Christ of the Indian Road*, 141–42.

49 Ibid., 148.

50 Taylor, *Contribution of Jones*, 11.

51 E. Stanley Jones, *Christ at the Round Table* (Nashville: Abingdon, 1928), 16.

52 Jones, *Christ of the Indian Road*, 193.

53 Ibid., 194.

54 Jones, *Song of Ascents*, 110.

55 Jones, *Christ at the Round Table*, 81.

56 Jones, *Song of Ascents*, 135.

57 E. Stanley Jones, *Christian Maturity* (Nashville: Abingdon Press, 1957), 173.

58 Jones, *Conversion*, 42.

59 Andrew F. Walls, "The Mission of the Church Today in the Light of Global History," *Word and World* 20, no. 1 (2000): 21.

60 Glen H. Stassen, "A New Vision," in *Authentic Transformation: A New Vision of Christ and Culture*, ed. Glen H. Stassen, D. M. Yeager, and John H. Yoder (Nashville: Abingdon Press, 1996), 230.

61 E. Stanley Jones, *The Divine Yes* (Nashville: Abingdon, 1975), 35.

62 Jones, *Christ at the Round Table*, 80.

Chapter 4

1 Pew Research Center, "America's Changing Religious Landscape" (May 12, 2015), 3. Mainline Protestant and Roman Catholic affiliation fell a combined 6.5 percent from making up a total of 42 percent of the population in 2007 to only 35.5 percent in 2014. During the same period, people who were unaffiliated with any religion increased by 6.7 percent, up to 22.8 percent of the population.

2 Bob Smietana, "Research: Unchurched Will Talk about Faith; Not Interested in Going to Church," LifeWay Research (June 28, 2016), http://lifewayresearch .com/2016/06/28/unchurched-will-talk-about-faith-not-interested-in-going-to -church/.

3 E. Stanley Jones, *The Christ of the Indian Road* (Nashville: Abingdon Press, 1953), 11–12.

4 E. Stanley Jones, *Christ at the Round Table* (Nashville: Abingdon Press, 1928), 19.

5 Ibid., 20.

6 Ibid., 20–21, emphasis original.

7 Ibid., 20.

8 Ibid., 21–22.

9 Ibid., 22.

10 Ibid., 23 (Note: The original groups were all men).

11 Ibid., 26.

12 William M. Pickard Jr., *Offer Them Christ: Christian Mission for the Twenty-First Century* (Franklin, TN: Providence House, 1998), 122–23.

13 Jones, *Christ at the Round Table*, 20–21.

14 Pickard, *Offer Them Christ*, 126.

15 Ibid.

16 "A New Generation Expresses Its Skepticism and Frustration with Christianity," Barna (September 21, 2007), https://www.barna.org/barna-update/millennials /94-a-new-generation-expresses-its-skepticism-and-frustration-with-christianity.

17 "Population by religion, sex and urban/rural residence – India," UNdata (2001), http://data.un.org/Data.aspx?d=POP&f=tableCode%3a28%3bcountryCode

%3a356&c=2,3,6,8,10,12,14,15,16&s=_countryEnglishNameOrderBy:asc,ref
Year:desc,areaCode:asc&v=1.

18 Douglas Ruffle, *A Missionary Mindset: What Church Leaders Need to Know to Reach Their Community, Lessons from E. Stanley Jones* (Nashville: Discipleship Resources, 2016), 77.

19 Lisa Green, "Americans Believe Church Is Good but Dying," LifeWay Research (March 30, 2015), http://lifewayresearch.com/2015/03/30/americans-believe -church-is-good-but-dying/.

20 Ruffle, *A Missionary Mindset*, 77.

21 Jones, *Christ at the Round Table*, 23.

22 Ibid., 24.

23 Ibid., 25.

24 Ibid., 328, emphasis original.

25 "So let no one boast about human leaders. For all things are yours, whether Paul or Apollos or Cephas or the world or life or death or the present or the future—all belong to you, and you belong to Christ, and Christ belongs to God" (NRSV).

26 Jones, *Christ at the Round Table*, 305.

27 Ibid., 67.

28 Ibid., 69.

29 Ibid., 295.

30 Ibid., 200.

31 Ibid., 192–93.

32 Ibid., 185.

33 Kenda Creasy Dean, *Almost Christian: What the Faith of Our Teenagers Is Telling the American Church* (New York: Oxford University, 2010), 131–56.

34 There is a growing set of literature helping with this, including James Choung's *True Story*, and my own book *Evangelism for Non-Evangelists*.

35 Jones, *Christ at the Round Table*, 133.

36 Ibid., 168.

37 Ibid., 308.

38 Ibid., 308–9.

39 Ibid., 309.

40 Ibid., 169.

41 Ibid., 71.

42 Ibid., 72.

Chapter 5

1 E. Stanley Jones, *A Song of Ascents: A Spiritual Autobiography* (Nashville: Abingdon Press, 1968), 233.

2 Ibid., 220.

3 E. Stanley Jones, *Along the Indian Road* (Nashville: Abingdon Press, 1939), 189.

4 Stephen A. Graham, *Ordinary Man, Extraordinary Mission: The Life and Work of E. Stanley Jones* (Nashville: Abingdon, 2005), 192.

5 Jones, *Song of Ascents*, 221. The acquisition of the property is a miracle story, and the formation of the Christian Ashram was a joint effort by Brother Stanley; the Rev. Yunas Sinha, an Indian clergyman; and Ethel Turner, a retired member of the London Missionary Society. "Three nationalities came together in that humble beginning—Indian, English, and American. It was a humble beginning. We hadn't the slightest idea that we were beginning something that would become a world movement," (215).

6 Ibid., 222.

7 Ibid.

8 Ibid.

9 Ibid., 215.

10 Ibid.

11 Ibid., 220. The Rev. Charles Kinder, in a personal interview, described his conversation with Jones, helping him see the importance of allowing others to serve as the evangelist for the Christian Ashram.

12 In addition to the retreat settings, Jones began to experiment with one-day and weekend, church-based Christian Ashrams in the 1960s. He was constantly willing to let the Holy Spirit adapt the structure to serve the mission—where it proved effective, he would continue the practice. Where the adaptations did not bear fruit, he was willing to learn and move forward.

13 Jones, *Song of Ascents*, 224.

14 Ibid., 227.

15 Ibid., 226, 228. The same information is provided to leaders in a document called the "10 Pillars of a Christian Ashram" and explained in detail for new participants in the handout "Orientation to a Christian Ashram."

16 Ibid., 205.

17 The original document written by E. Stanley Jones is contained in the Asbury Seminary Archives, quoted here from Anne Mathews-Younes' unpublished manuscript, "A History of the Christian Ashram in North America," page 1 of the section "The Restructuring Decade—1950–1960."

18 "(1) Jesus Christ is the apex, the Guru of the Ashram. (2) The Three made up of J. T. Seamands, William Berg, and myself are the working executive of The Seven. (3) The Seven is the group which has inherited the United Christian Ashrams, Incorporated, in Texas as a nonprofit organization. The Seven directs the movement, decides its personnel, and holds the property. I am the chairman of the Seven, but "The Seven" is the authoritative body. When I pass on, The Seven will elect another chairman and the movement goes on. The local Ashrams approved of the transfer of authority from me, as the founder, to The Seven. (4) The Twelve is the group which runs the local Ashrams. It is made up of nine local people, plus The Three. The Three, representing the whole, are there to see that the local Ashrams do not depart from the basic

principles and procedures; otherwise the local Twelve run the local Ashrams. (5) The One Hundred and Twenty (the number in the Upper Room at Pentecost) is the Family Meeting which meets daily during the Ashram session and decides suggestions for improvement or change. The Twelve are approved by the Family Meeting and are the executive group of it, to act in-between Ashrams. (6) The Five Hundred Brethren—the Ashram Associates—are the financial and sustaining basic of the Ashrams. Those who give $5 or more per year and who work and pray for the Ashrams are Associates. (7) The church is the home of us all. The movement is interdenominational but deeply church-centered. We try to send back our members into their respective churches as better pastors, members, and officials" (E. Stanley Jones quoted in Younes, "A History of the Christian Ashram in North America," p. 1 of the section "The Restructuring Decade—1950–1960").

19 Ibid.
20 Jones, *Song of Ascents*, 233.
21 Graham, *Ordinary Man, Extraordinary Mission*, 354.

Chapter 6

1 Private conversation.
2 C. Daniel Batson, "Orchestrating Prosocial Motives," in *Moral Leadership: The Theory and Practice of Power, Judgment, and Policy*, ed. Deborah L. Rhode (Hoboken, NJ: Jossey-Bass, 2006), 197.
3 Rob Davis, "Advocacy Part II: Definitions," accessed September 5, 2016, http://place.asburyseminary.edu/cgi/viewcontent.cgi?article=1013&context=advocacypapers.
4 Ibid.
5 Batson, "Orchestrating Prosocial Motives," 210.
6 Stephen A. Graham, *Ordinary Man, Extraordinary Mission: The Life and Work of E. Stanley Jones* (Nashville: Abingdon, 2005), 61, 111.
7 John Wesley, Sermon 63, "The General Spread of the Gospel," from *Sermons II*, ed. Albert C. Outler, *The Bicentennial Edition of The Works of John Wesley*, vol. 2 (Nashville: Abingdon, 1976–), 485–99.
8 Graham, *Ordinary Man, Extraordinary Mission*, 113.
9 E. Stanley Jones, *A Song of Ascents: A Spiritual Autobiography* (Nashville: Abingdon Press, 1968), 132.
10 E. Stanley Jones, *The Christ of the Indian Road* (Nashville: Abingdon Press, 2014), 36; eBook Collection (EBSCOhost), EBSCOhost, accessed November 2, 2016.
11 Jones, *Christ of the Indian Road*, 121.
12 Jones, *Song of Ascents*, 159–60.
13 E. Stanley Jones, "Unshakable Kingdom: Three Notes in the Song of Ascents," Asbury Theological Seminary Chapel Services (1968), accessed August 3, 2016, http://place.asburyseminary.edu/ecommonsatchapelservices/4652/.

14 Jones, *Song of Ascents*, 108.

15 E. Stanley Jones, "What Is America's Role in This Crisis?," *The Christian Century* (March 19, 1941): 388.

16 Ibid.

17 Ibid.

18 E. Stanley Jones, "An Open Letter to Japan," Asbury Theological Seminary, B. L. Fisher Library Special Collections, Papers of E. Stanley Jones ARC2000-007, box 24, folder 1.

19 E. Stanley Jones, "Letter to President Franklin D. Roosevelt," January 5, 1942, Asbury Theological Seminary, B. L. Fisher Library Special Collections, Papers of E. Stanley Jones ARC2000-007, box 3, folder 7.

20 Ibid.

21 E. Stanley Jones, "Letter to John Foster Dulles from ESJ (in Tokyo)," February 8, 1953, Asbury Theological Seminary, B. L. Fisher Library Special Collections, Papers of E. Stanley Jones ARC2000-007, box 5, folder 2.

22 "Report of the Office of Censorship," Office of Censorship: United States of America, June 10, 1943, Asbury Theological Seminary, B. L. Fisher Library Special Collections, Papers of E. Stanley Jones ARC2000-007, box 62, folder 1.

23 Claude G. Bowers, "Report on the Speeches Made by Dr. Eli Stanley Jones in Santiago, Chile," May 24, 1945, Asbury Theological Seminary, B. L. Fisher Library Special Collections, Papers of E. Stanley Jones ARC2000-007, box 62, folder 1.

24 Jones, *Song of Ascents*, 395.

25 E. Stanley Jones, *The Unshakable Kingdom and the Unchanging Person* (Bellingham, WA: McNett, 1995), throughout.

Chapter 7

1 E. Stanley Jones, *The Christ of the Indian Road* (Nashville: Abingdon Press, digital edition, 2014), 83.

2 "2015 Sees Sharp Rise in Post-Christian Population," Barna (August 12, 2015), https://www.barna.com/research/2015-sees-sharp-rise-in-post-christian-population/.

3 "Meet the Spiritual but Not Religious," Barna (April 6, 2017), https://www.barna.com/research/2015-sees-sharp-rise-in-post-christian-population/.

4 David Kinnaman and Gabe Lyons, *Unchristian: What a New Generation Really Thinks About Christianity . . . And Why It Matters* (Grand Rapids, MI: Baker Books, 2007).

5 Jones, *Christ of the Indian Road*, 17.

6 Ibid., 21.

7 "Graham Disinvited from Prayer Event over Islam Comments," CNN, April 23, 2010, http://www.cnn.com/2010/US/04/23/graham.islam.controversy/.

8 Kimberly D. Reisman, *Embrace: The Essence of Authentic Evangelism* (Franklin, TN: Seedbed, publication pending).

9 David J. Bosch, *Transforming Mission: Paradigm Shifts in Theology of Mission* (Maryknoll, NY: Orbis Books, 1991), 489.

10 Jones, *Christ of the Indian Road*, 21, emphasis added.

11 Ibid., 120.

12 Ibid., 49.

13 Ibid., 8.

14 Ibid., 63.

15 Ibid., 64.

16 Ibid., 103.

17 Ibid., 118–19, emphasis added.

18 Ibid.

19 Ibid., 112.

20 Ibid., 119.

21 Ibid., 11.

22 Wikipedia, s.v. "Discovery Doctrine," last modified December 3, 2017, 17:18, https://en.wikipedia.org/wiki/Discovery_doctrine.

23 Jones, *Christ of the Indian Road*, 134.

24 Eddie Fox and George Morris, *Faith Sharing: Dynamic Christian Witnessing by Invitation* (Nashville: Discipleship Resources, 1996), 104–105.

25 Bob Smietana, "Research: Unchurched Will Talk about Faith, Not Interested in Going to Church," Lifeway Research (June 28, 2016), http://lifewayresearch.com/2016/06/28/unchurched-will-talk-about-faith-not-interested-in-going-to-church/.

26 Jones, *Christ of the Indian Road*, 131.

27 Ibid., 131–32.

28 Smietana, "Unchurched Will Talk."

Conclusion

1 Jack Jackson covers this well in the introduction.